CHESH
Villages

Text by the Cheshire Federation of Women's Institutes
Photographs by Bill Meadows

COUNTRYSIDE BOOKS
Newbury, Berkshire

COUNTRYSIDE BOOKS
3 Catherine Road
Newbury, Berkshire

To view our complete range of books,
Please visit us at
www.countrysidebooks.co.uk

ISBN 1 85306 688 5

The front cover photograph is of Great Budworth
and the back cover photograph shows detail of the
Lewis Carroll memorial window at All Saints church, Daresbury

Designed by Graham Whiteman

Produced through MRM Associates Ltd., Reading
Printed in Italy

FOREWORD

T his all-colour book is a celebration of some of Cheshire's most photogenic villages. Along with superb pictures by landscape photographer Bill Meadows, it brings together many of the accounts of village life contained in *The Cheshire Village Book*, first published in 1990. These accounts portray a fascinating picture of life, past and present, in village communities and illustrate how important a role small, rural communities play in the overall scheme of things. This importance continues in the early years of the new century at a time when some areas are losing their local distinctiveness.

Cheshire has such a wonderfully diverse character from the sea and sand of the Wirral coast, through rich agricultural land to the foothills of the Pennines. The villages in these areas offer an opportunity for the visitor and resident alike to explore and enjoy a wealth of interest and to experience the delight of the unexpected.

Come and share the magic of Cheshire in all its variety.

Maureen Walmsley
Chairman
Cheshire Federation of Women's Institutes
Autumn 2001

View of Bollington

⌘ ACTON

Throughout the last four centuries Acton has been dominated by its seats of power. – Dorfold Hall (1621) and Woodhey, a greater house standing, alas no more, at Burland. All that remains of the latter is a chapel erected in 1700 by Lady Wilbraham. Interesting features of it apart from its elaborate wooden carvings and high-backed pews, are its brickwork passages, 7 ft high. The remaining Dorfold Hall with its iron gates and majestic drive, is a delight to the motorist on the A534 Chester to Nantwich road. The Spanish chestnut tree in its grounds is thought to be the last tree remaining of Delamere Forest in this area – its age reputed to be 1,000 years.

As one approaches Acton village from any one of three directions, the sense of history is enhanced by the rise of the 800 year old tower of St Mary's. It is mother church to five others, including the pretty St Mary's in Nantwich, some two miles distant. Originally established by monks from Combermere Abbey in 1180, it was used as a safe house in the skirmishes with the Welsh. Its font, rescued from a farmyard, is decorated with a man and a hare-like animal, both reputed older than Domesday. Its figures of William Mainwaring, recumbent for 600 years, and Sir Richard Wilbraham in 17th century armour, lie within.

From here the siege of Nantwich was directed. In fact it was used as a garrison by the Royalists and fighting actually took place within the church. Some say that the turning point of the Civil War was the battle fought at Acton and Dorfold, on 25th January 1644. Women took part in the battle and 120 were taken prisoner. As a result of these troubles the vicar, Rev Lowe, is reputed to have buried the altar vessels for safety. His secret went with him to the grave and the vessels are yet undiscovered.

⌘ ALDERLEY EDGE

Alderley Edge is a small village and well-known Cheshire beauty spot, approximately 14 miles south of Manchester and 18 miles north of Crewe. Until the middle of the 19th century, it was called Chorley or Chorleigh, but later the name was changed to Alderley Edge. One notable exception is Chorley Hall (about half a mile from the village).

The village lies under the shadow of Castle Rock, a large projecting rock roughly 650 ft above sea level. Visitors come all year round to wander through the wood and enjoy the fine view of the Cheshire Plain from the Rock.

There are a number of caves, the result of tunnelling underground in search of copper. The entrance to these caves was approximately half a mile from Castle Rock and the sand extracted from the workings formed two large sandhills where years ago the village children could spend the day playing quite safely. Several unsuccessful attempts have been made to work the mines.

Looking over Alderley Edge

Two more caves are situated in an area of the woods known as Stormy Point. The entrance to one (known as the Devil's Grave) is narrow and legend says that if anyone walked round it seven times and repeated the Lord's Prayer backwards, the Devil would appear. The other cave has a large open entrance and again legend says it was once occupied by an army of 40 warriors and 40 white horses, who, should the country be plunged into war, would be there to defend us. Their leader was called the Wizard and a small hotel of that name is still there.

There were three hotels in the village, the Trafford Arms, the Queen's Hotel (now offices) and the Royal Oak, and a small inn originally called the Drum and Monkey. Again, legend decrees, should the country be involved in war – 'the

Wizard would bring his army, the Queen's Hotel the Charter sign, the Oak would give the Royal Command and the Drum would beat the time!'

When the railway came to Alderley, Manchester businessmen, chiefly cotton merchants, were persuaded by the railway company to build houses here. A number of very large houses were built, whose owners were rewarded by a silver medallion (worn by the gentlemen on their watch chains) entitling them to free first class travel to and from Manchester for a number of years. These families provided work for the poorer villagers, who were employed as servants, gardeners, coachmen and butlers.

⌘ ANTROBUS

The village lies off the A559 Warrington/Northwich road. People named Antrobus take their name from the village, which is the only one so called in England and

The gardens at Arley Hall, near Antrobus

appears in the Domesday Book as Enterbus or Entrebus – 'between the thickets'. Foggs Lane is thought to be an old Roman road, although this has not been proved.

In spite of this, Antrobus is of more modern times. The church, the Church of England school and the Methodist chapel were all built in the 19th century, also the majority of the houses. The oldest is of cruck construction, known as Broom Cottage.

The earliest place of worship and the most interesting historically is the Friends' Meeting House, Sevenoaks, Frandley. George Fox is reputed to have preached under an oak tree nearby, one of seven, all of which have now died.

Major Arnold Boyd, the great Cheshire naturalist, lived in the village and was well known for his natural history books of the area. Major Boyd also helped to revive the soul caking play which is still performed every year on or near All Souls' Day in nearby inns etc, although in earlier decades they went from house to house performing the old verses.

An area of land was set aside in 1854 for 'Allotments for the Labouring Poor', administered by the Parish Council. In the 1980s this land was sold and the money invested by the new Antrobus Relief in Need Charity, using the interest to help present day residents.

The names of fields, woods etc are fascinating and intriguing – Grandsire's Green, Cobblers Gorse, Shutterduck Meadow, Hades' Nook, Tinklers Field, The Folly, Newalls Rough, Bang'em Lane (now Occupation Road), Gypsy Field, the Pleasure Ground.

⌘ APPLETON THORN

Appleton Thorn, in the Domesday Book as Elpletune, is the village central to a wide area known as Appleton. In 1178 the landowner was Adam de Dutton, an ancestor of the Egerton Warburton family of Arley. It was he who set up Appleton Cross, the steps of which still remain, and brought and planted the original thorn tree which gave the village its name.

The tree was said to have been an offshot of the Glastonbury thorn which grew from the staff of Joseph of Arimathea. This is thought to be the only place in England where the 'Bawning of the Thorn' still takes place, always in the middle of June. The tree is decorated with flowers and ribbons and children dance round it in the style of a maypole chanting verses to the tune of *Bonnie Dundee*, each followed by the chorus:

> 'Up with fresh garlands this midsummer morn,
> Up with red ribbons on Appleton Thorn.
> Come lasses and lads to the Thorn Tree today
> To bawm it and shout as yet bawm it "Hurray"!'

Much traffic now passes through the village as the road links the M56 and M6 motorways to the large industrial estate established on the site of the war-time naval airfield, then known as HMS Black Cap. Also on this site but within the village, opposite the school, stands the prison, first opened in November 1960 as an open prison for mild offenders and now, following an £8,000,000 rebuilding scheme, known as Thorn Cross Youth Custody Centre. Integration with the village has been good and it is possible to hold events within its walls.

There are thatched cottages in Chapel Lane and Pepper Street and the post office alongside the prison gates has a Dickensian appearance.

The Appleton Thorn Potato Exchange was established here in the early 1930s. Farmers brought their produce and merchants came from Wigan and other areas to agree a price. In 1940 this exchange was officially stopped by the Ministry but farmers still met three times a week to agree a price and continued to do so until the 1980s, when it finally ceased. The land opposite the thorn was then sold and the money invested to provide a scholarship for research into potato husbandry.

⌘ ASTBURY

The village of Astbury lies two and a half miles south-west of the Cheshire town of Congleton. Evidence of a Roman settlement lies in the discovery over 200 years ago of the remains of a Roman camp, and the even earlier history of the village can be

Astbury churchyard

traced back to the Bronze Age, strikingly illustrated by the site of a cremation and burial ground. A further remarkable discovery was that of a dug-out canoe found in the bed of a stream in the village in the 1920s.

The triangular village green, daffodil-covered in spring, and surrounded by picturesque cottages, is crowned by the ancient parish church of St Mary and provides one of the most photographed scenes in Cheshire. A fine Queen Anne rectory, village hall, the Church of England school for 100 children, built in 1843, with a village store, post office and inn and small groups of houses and farms complete the village scene.

The parish of Astbury lies on the edge of the Cheshire Plain, rising from the village through farmland and woodland to the moorland ridge recognised as an extremity of the Pennine range, leading to Mow Cop and the boundary with Staffordshire. The 1,000 ft high ridge commands admired views westwards over the Cheshire Plain to the distant Welsh hills and eastwards to the Staffordshire and Derbyshire moors.

Astbury's Gothic church, with its unusual feature of a detached tower and steeple, dates back to the 14th century. Its origins lie in the original church mentioned in the Domesday Book. A further link in the history of the village is provided by the 1,000 year old yew tree in the churchyard, its leafy branches spreading above the shell of its hollow trunk.

The parish has never lacked 'characters', amongst them a past resident who claimed to have the longest beard which, at a length of 11 ft, he is reputed to have hung over an apple bough to dry after washing! Not only human but animal records emerge, amongst them one from the year 1774 of what is claimed to be the heaviest pig ever recorded. Clearly an imposing animal, it is reported as standing 4 ft 8 inches high, 9 ft 8 inches in length and weighing-in at 12 cwt.

⌘ AUDLEM

Audlem, the most southerly township in Cheshire, is noted in the Domesday Book as Aldelime, deriving from Alda, a personal name, and lyme, a forest. The parish includes the ancient coaching and market town of Audlem and also the townships of Buerton and Hankelow.

The Shropshire Union Canal, once used to carry the local cheese to Liverpool and Birmingham, now carries upwards of 60,000 visitors through the village each summer and the old canal warehouse on the wharf is now a public house catering for the needs of those who have worked through the 15 locks which bring the canal from Shropshire down to the Cheshire Plain!

The church of St James the Great was built in 1278 and dominates the centre of Audlem from its position on a large mound. The old butter cross stands below the church steps and beside it is the bear stone, a large granite boulder which still shows where the ring was attached to which bears were tied for baiting at the local Wakes.

The church of St James the Great dominates Audlem

The free grammar school, now an old people's home, was built in 1655 with money raised locally, to teach classics and English grammar to boys. It ended its educational life as a secondary modern school in the late 1960s. Geoffrey Whitney, an Elizabethan poet and author of *Choice of Emblemes*, was born at nearby Coole Pilate. One of his emblems is dedicated 'to the youth at the school of Audlem in England'. The school he refers to pre-dated the grammar school.

Hankelow, a mile from Audlem on the road to Nantwich, is a lively community, keeping the green with its ponds and ducks as an attractive centrepiece.

⌘ BARNSTON

Barnston appears in the Domesday Book as Bernestone, then held by William Fitz-Nigel, second Baron of Halton. Barnston used to be part of the parish of

Woodchurch. There is a board in Woodchurch church recording that 'James Goodyker of Barnston in the parish of Woodchurch died in the Year of our Lord 1525, left 20 Marks to buy 20 Yoke of Bullocks, which were afterwards, by order of the Commissioners of Pious Uses, converted into Cows and given to the poor of the said Parish'. Barnston's Christ church is of recent origin, 1871.

The buildings in the village which surround the green are of the 18th and 19th centuries. A cobbled lane leads from the green to the rear of the churchyard and some of the cottages there are much older. Behind the church are earthworks which are the remains of the earlier village.

In Barnston Dale is a very ancient watercourse, the Ayne, which eventually joins the Fender. There is said to have been a watermill here. A Richard of Barnston, miller, is recorded in 1376. There is also a well which was in use until just before the First World War.

The public house, the Fox and Hounds which dates from the 16th century is in the Dale. Its previous names have been The Flag, The Hen and Chickens and The Black Horse.

Part of Bank Farm was a tollgate cottage with gates onto a turnpike road. Houses in Storeton Lane preserve the names of the fields in which they were built – The Longcroft, The Woodcroft and The Aynecroft.

Today the land use is predominantly agricultural, although the population is mainly composed of urban commuters.

⌘ BARROW

The parish consists of Great and Little Barrow with the hamlets of Broomhill, Stamford Bridge and the areas of Long Green and Hollowmore Heath, and lies between two main highways about four miles from the centre of Chester city.

The village lies on and around a low sandstone hill running north to south. The bedrock gives rise to the most typical feature of Barrow – the lanes cut through the rock and the many sandstone walls.

Stamford Bridge (formerly Stone Ford) was an important ford on the river Gowy in prehistoric times and the Romans used this crossing when they constructed Watling Street – the route of which still forms the southern boundary of the village.

By 1291 there was a church at Barrow and there is a complete list of rectors from 1313. It was extensively remodelled and refurbished in the 1880s.

Many of the older houses in the village were or still are farms. Most date from the 17th and 18th centuries and several houses contain beams which are said to have come from ships broken up in the Dee shipbreakers' yards.

Barrowmore Hall was built in 1879/81 for Hugh Lyle Smyth of Liverpool. It was an impressive residence designed by John Douglas, the noted Chester church architect, with landscaped gardens containing specimen and unusual trees which still thrive. In 1920 it became the East Lancashire Tuberculosis Colony, which developed into Barrowmore Village Settlement – providing work, homes, rehabilitation and training for disabled people. The sanatorium based in the former Barrowmore Hall was completely destroyed by a landmine in 1940 with the deaths of 32 patients and staff. In 1947 the NHS acquired the hospital premises and it became Barrowmore Hospital.

⌘ BARTHOMLEY

Barthomley, with St Bertoline's church in the background

Little is known of Barthomley before late Saxon and early Norman times. Formerly the church was the centre of a parish of considerable area and included Barthomley, Balterley, Crewe (Crewe Green), Alsager and Haslington. Now only the first two 'townships' remain.

Some customs of the past include a curfew rung at eight o'clock from Michaelmas to Lady Day; and the 'Pancake Bell' on Shrove Tuesday, which was significantly known locally as 'Guttit' Tuesday (Good Tide Tuesday). Also, daily at one o'clock, a bell was rung to summon the farm workers back to their work.

'The Old Rectory', originally 'The Hall', was a large three-storeyed house built in Georgian style. Some years ago the top storey was removed, making it more manageable. Doing this ended the traditional ghost story of the spirit of Randle Crewe, which at the witching hour of night visited the top storey, walking the passages clanking chains.

There is a legend that the last wolf killed in England was actually caught in a wood in Barthomley, hence 'Wulvarn', the name of the brook running through the village.

The church, St Bertoline's, has been called the 'Church of the Massacre', in consequence of a tragic occurrence in the Civil War. A number of villagers led, it has been said, by the son of the rector, who had fired on the Royalist army advancing from Nantwich, took refuge in the church tower. They were smoked out and twelve were massacred. It may be a significant fact that the parish register of this date has been mutilated.

The attractive White Lion Inn near the church must surely be one of the most quaint in Cheshire. It is a black and white thatched building dating from the 16th century. According to old records, it was previously the home of the parish clerk and was not used as an inn until the latter part of the 19th century.

⌘ BEESTON

The village of Beeston is dominated by the castle, which is situated on a pyramid-shaped crag, with magnificent views of the surrounding countryside. It was originally occupied in the Bronze Age, became an Iron Age fort which was then destroyed by the Romans. In the 13th century it became a key point among the border strongholds.

The castle has a 360 ft deep well. It was in this well that Richard II's treasure, valued at 20,000 marks, is reputed to have been stored, before it was surrendered to Henry Bolingbroke. Later, during the Civil War, the castle was used for storing arms and for safe keeping of the local gentry's valuables.

In 1959 the castle was taken over by the Ministry of Works, now the Department of the Environment, and some excavation and restoration has been carried out. It is a popular place for families to visit.

The Image House is an old cottage, so named because of the images of faces on

The view from Beeston Castle

the front of the cottage. It has a legend of having been built in a night in the days when if a man could 'fashion a dwelling and have smoke coming out of the chimney by the morning', he could call it his own.

Present day interest in the village is maintained by a thriving cattle market held each Wednesday and Friday and a lively and colourful general market every Bank Holiday Monday to which people travel from miles around.

The first Outdoor Education Centre in Cheshire was opened at Beeston, close to the castle, in 1970.

⌘ BOLLINGTON

The original settlement of Bollington comprised Lowerhouse, Bollington Cross and Kerridge to the east, with its quarries and stonemasons, and there is evidence of a pre-industrial, working community. It was not until the opening of the Lowerhouse Mill by Samuel Greg, son of the owner of the now well-known Quarry Bank Mill at Styal, that the development of Bollington started along the narrow valley to the north-east.

Looking down on Bollington from Kerridge Hill

The opening of the canal in 1831, and the coming of the railway in 1870 made it possible for an increase in every aspect of the trade development, and the hamlets of Bollington Cross, Lowerhouse and Kerridge joined into the industrial town which is still called a village to this day. In 1848 Slaters' Lancashire and Cheshire Directory recorded Bollington as 'A thriving village with some collieries and extensive cotton factories.' In the first half of the 19th century the population increased from 1,200 to just over 4,600.

Meanwhile Kerridge continued with its quarrying, as it is still doing with some distinction. The cathedral at Coventry is paved with Kerridge stone.

The damp climate and soft water suited the spinning of the finest quality Egyptian cotton, and for many years the best Liberty cottons were woven in Bollington.

Situated at the foothills of the adjacent Peak District, and with the good fortune to have beautiful views from almost every dwelling and street corner, Bollington has many attractions. The stone cottages are built to withstand the climate – fierce winds sweeping over the Derbyshire Peaks and early snow on the heights of Kerridge.

⌘ BOSLEY

Mentioned in the Domesday Book as Boselega, Bosley is a small but somewhat scattered village with a population of approximately 350, nestling at the foot of the Pennines and five miles south of Macclesfield. Lying on the verge of the county and separated from Staffordshire by the river Dane, it is mostly a sheep and dairy farming district. The Cloud, which is actually in Staffordshire, dominates the village and is the penultimate peak of the Pennine chain.

Bosley Works, which is a large sprawling establishment at the foot of the Cloud, was originally built on the orders of Charles Roe as a copper rolling and hammering works, together with 19 cottages for the workers. With the help of James Brindley, he harnessed the power of the river Dane. The works were later converted into two cotton mills and around 1860 they were occupied by three corn millers and a silk throwster, but from the early 1920s to the present time it has been and still is a very busy wood flour treatment works employing around 120 people.

The church of St Mary is a small edifice with nave and chancel and is built of brick, except the tower which is of stone, low and embattled, and which was part of a former church built around 1300. This was destroyed by fire and was rebuilt in 1777. The Methodist church in Tunstall Road was built in 1885 and replaced the Wesleyan chapel which had stood at Bosley Works since 1832.

Higher up from the chapel is Key Green Farm where alterations uncovered old beams, wattle walls and a fireplace with the date 1610 and the initials RB and IB engraved in the sandstone. These are reputed to be the initials of members of the Broster family, which originally came to Bosley after crossing from France with

Bosley Locks on the Macclesfield Canal

William the Conqueror. Their name in those days was Brostirre, and descendants of the family still reside elsewhere in the village.

Bosley reservoir, built by Messrs Tredwell in 1832, is a fine stretch of water covering upwards of 120 acres. It supports abundant wildlife and was built as a feeder to the Macclesfield Canal, which was engineered by Thomas Telford and which opened in 1831. Canal users are only too familiar with the twelve locks which have to be traversed on this stretch of the canal.

⌘ BOSTOCK

The village of Bostock is situated on the Middlewich/Northwich road and villagers have always claimed Bostock to be the centre of the county. There has been an oak tree on the village green for many generations to mark the exact spot – the present tree was planted by Canon Thomas France-Hayhurst and Col C. H. France-Hayhurst in 1887, the Golden Jubilee year of Queen Victoria's reign.

The village has a long history. The Domesday Book records Bostock as being held by Osmer, a Saxon, whose family later took the name of Bostock and lived here for generations.

Bostock parish consists of estate farms and cottages for the estate workers. These buildings are constructed of red brick and have attractive black and white gables. The distinctive red bricks were made from clay extracted on the site and fired in a kiln situated in what is still known as Brick Kiln Lane.

Records show that in 1824 there were five cottages belonging to the overseer of the poor, housing families dependent upon parish relief.

In 1905 the estate laundry was built on the village green, in which was done the washing from the Hall. Reading rooms for the estate workers were housed in a pleasant building facing the green. Times change, and the laundry is now the village hall, frequently used by the community. The reading rooms became a social club for the estate employees and in recent years membership has been extended to include people living outside the village. Facing the village green is the attractive workshop of the village 'blacksmith', now known as an agricultural engineer.

Bostock is a small but active community. In the early part of the 20th century land was given to the villagers by Col W. H. France-Hayhurst to provide a bowling green, tennis courts and sports pavilion with a grass play area, and these facilities are still well used.

⌘ BRERETON

The village which centres around Brereton Hall and the church of St Oswald, on the banks of the river Croco, lies in a fertile agricultural area, with natural resources which have greatly influenced its development. Although the finding of a box of Roman coins near Brindley Moors Farm in 1820, and the Anglo-Saxon derivation of the actual name, suggests that a settlement existed prior to the Norman Conquest, there is no recorded mention of the 'manor of Bretune' until the Domesday Book.

The existing Hall, a Grade I listed building which is approached through the lodge gates built in 1800, was constructed during the reign of Elizabeth I by Sir William Brereton.

The adjacent church dedicated to St Oswald dates from the 15th century and has a square tower with five bells, rung from the ground floor. It is believed that one of the Breretons who had fought in the Crusades pledged to build the church in gratitude for a safe return.

Evidence of the village's continued importance to travellers is the Bear's Head, a black and white 'magpie' coaching inn, dated 1615. It carries as its sign the head of a muzzled bear, which was the traditional emblem of the Brereton family. Legend has it that Sir William was interrupted, while dining, by his valet, and in his anger pursued and subsequently murdered him. In remorse Sir William travelled to London to crave pardon from the King. He was detained in the Tower of London, his life being spared on condition that he designed an effective muzzle for a bear! When confronted by the bear, the creature was successfully muzzled, Sir William was duly pardoned and the muzzled bear's head became the family emblem.

Where water once provided power for Brereton mill and for agriculture, it is now proving to be a leisure attraction. An area of estate land which was unproductive and remained as heath and woodland, was transformed with the discovery of pure silica sand in 1959. The topsoil removed, the quarrying proceeded for more than ten years providing sand for industry, glassmaking and cosmetics. Then after it had lain dormant until 1981, the Borough Council purchased the land and the Country Park was created.

⌘ BRIDGEMERE

In medieval times Bridgemere boasted a bloomery or iron foundry. Included in this district are the hamlets of Doddington and Hunsterson. It is a scattering of farms, houses and cottages and typical Cheshire scenery of open fields, woods and copses.

On the Doddington estate in the midst of farmland stands a red sandstone castle, the remains of the crenellated manor house built in 1364 by Sir John Delves. The Delves family, or as it later became Delves Broughton, remained on the estate for many years; however the Hall was used as a school until recently and is now private apartments.

A short drive, known as Wilbraham's Walk, through the main lodge gates passing one side of the lake, brings one to Doddington Hall. This house, built between 1777 and 1797 to the design of Samuel Wyatt, in the English Renaissance style, is of grey Portland stone. A magnificent sweep of stone steps, reputed to be the work of Adam, leads to the main entrance.

A tragic murder took place in the Chapel Field, Hunsterson on the night of 28th June 1835, when an elderly married man, Thomas Bagguley, strangled 15 year old Mary Malpas, throwing her body into Chapel Pool. Later he committed suicide in the stables of Doddington Cottage, where he had been employed. There are those who believe he haunts the stables still.

A few hundred yards from the school stands Bridgemere Hall and farm, which until 1989 had been in the Noden family for over 130 years. In 1972 Joe Noden, who had always had an interest in waterfowl and conservation, landscaped 30 acres and developed what became known as Bridgemere Wildlife Park.

Bridgemere Garden World was created in 1961, when John Ravenscroft with two assistants began what has become a 25 acre display of fascinating plants and gardens. Indoors is Europe's largest collection of house plants, a restaurant and well stocked shop. Over 140 people, many local, are employed in the growing areas and the centre itself.

⌘ BROXTON & BICKERTON

The Sandstone Trail winds its way across the Broxton and Bickerton hills, and walkers can look down into the villages and away across the Cheshire Plain.

The Maiden Castle site is visible, a stronghold of the Iron Age on the Broxton hill, while King James' Parlour, the cave reputed to have sheltered the monarch and his horse, is in the woods by the rebuilt Broxton Hall.

Friesian Holstein cattle are the predominant breed in this dairy farming area and this industry gives work to many. Several racing and breeding stables and other equine interests flourish around the foot of the hills.

The second Methodist chapel, erected in 1913, stands at the head of the Brown Knowl village, a fitting memorial to John Wedgwood, son of Josiah of Potteries fame, who brought Methodism to the area in 1822, and was finally laid to rest there as was his wish.

Holy Trinity church, Bickerton, nestles between the two hills, set within its own walled churchyard.

The copper mine 'chimney' stands tall against the hillside, a reminder of activities in bygone days; the tools and mining equipment on display in the Copper Mine public house are fascinating to see. The Bickerton Poacher public house is a venue for walkers, providing refreshment and entertainment, the indoor well reminding them of the abundance of water in the area.

⌘ BUNBURY

The old Saxon settlement surrounded an 8th century church dedicated to St Boniface. Sir Hugh de Calveley, renowned for his fighting in France and Spain,

Staircase Locks near Bunbury on the Shropshire Union Canal

instigated its 14th century re-modelling and established it as a collegiate church.

In 1527, Sir Ralph Egerton, Standard Bearer to Henry VIII, built a chantry chapel onto the south chancel of the church, and a chantry house nearby, for two priests who were to pray for his soul. Following the suppression of chantries by Henry VIII, it came into the possession of Thomas Aldersey, a wealthy merchant from Spurstow, who in 1594, obtained letters patent from Queen Elizabeth to establish a free grammar school for boys in the field next to the house, which then became a home for the headmaster, and also boarders.

Before he died, Thomas vested the school and house in the Worshipful Company of Haberdashers of which he was a member. In 1874, the school was demolished and a new one was built, but to this day, although now County Council-maintained and a mixed primary school, it is still owned by the Haberdashers' Company.

A few black and white houses remain. Because the village lay in the flight path of German bombers turned back by the barrage around Crewe, it was bombed several times during the Second World War.

Bunbury 'Wakes' originated centuries ago from the patronal festival of St Boniface. An old handbill of June 1808, states: 'Wanted, a person to conduct performances at Bunbury Wake, on 20th, 21st and 22nd instant. It is necessary that he should have a complete knowledge of pony and donkey racing: wheelbarrow, bag, cock and pigeon racing; archery, single-stick, quoits, cricket, football, cocking, wrestling, bull and badger baiting, dog fighting, goose riding, bumble puppy etc.' What could the 'etc' have been?

⌘ BURLEYDAM

The village, which was originally called Burledam, is situated on the Cheshire/Shropshire border, and it has been said that the real Burleydam consists of one house near the centre of the village. This stands between two brooks, the Burley and the Walkmill, both of which eventually join the river Weaver.

The church was built in 1769 by Sir Lynch Cotton and until 1869 it was the private chapel of Combermere Abbey. It then became the parish church. The Rev Thomas Meredyth was appointed the first vicar, having previously been private chaplain to Lord Combermere.

Combermere Abbey stands on the site of an old monastery, originally founded by Baron Hugh de Malbanc, of Nantwich, in 1133. It has been said that after the Dissolution of the Monasteries, the abbey bells were removed and taken to Wrenbury and are still there. Another version of the story is that the bells were thrown into the mere, a lake covering 132 acres and the largest in any private park in England.

The Combermere Arms is 450 years old and has solid oak doors and beautiful panelling. This well known hostelry is said to have been haunted by a ghost, but two clergymen persuaded it to enter into a bottle, which is buried under the entrance step. If this is ever broken the spirit will be released!

⌘ BURTON-IN-WIRRAL

Burton, a tun or settlement near a defended place (probably the Iron Age promontory fort just outside the village), is considered to be one of the most picturesque villages in Wirral.

The Domesday Book says 'there is a priest', but does not mention a church, which is not unusual. The church, dedicated to St Nicholas (the patron saint of sailors, because Burton was the port of Chester from about 1200 to 1500) was rebuilt in 1721 after the medieval church had fallen into disrepair. There was a Norman church and it is thought that there was an even earlier one.

Thomas Wilson was born in the village in 1663. He later became the Bishop of Sodor and Man and founded a school in 1724 'for the free education of Burton boys and girls and four from Puddington' (the next village about a mile away, in the same parish and sharing the same church).

For about 750 years Burton had an absentee landlord, who was the Bishop of Coventry and Lichfield, but in 1806 Richard Congreve became the first resident lord of the manor. In 1902 the estate passed to new owners and Henry Neville Gladstone became the new lord of the manor. He was the third son of the Prime

Burton-in-Wirral

Minister and he laid a sewer down the village street and later presented us with our village hall, known to this day as the 'GVH' (Gladstone Village Hall). In 1924 the manor estate of Burton was sold, not to a new lord of the manor, as believed by Mr Gladstone, but to a firm of estate agents, who sold off the land piecemeal as 'prime building land'.

However, the old world charm and feeling of tranquillity has been preserved, now that the village has been declared a conservation area. Just outside the village on Burton Hill are the remains of an old peg-mill built by the Massey family in 1629 and on the edge of the marsh on the Dee estuary are the even older remains of an ancient 'hospice', mentioned in a deed of 1293.

⌘ BURTONWOOD

Burtonwood is situated near the M6 and M62 between St Helens and Warrington. It is a village with tree-lined roads, the trees having been supplied by T. Forshaw of Burtonwood Brewery fame and planted by the schoolchildren.

In 1867 James Forshaw purchased the land on which the Burtonwood Brewery now stands, the trade then supplying free houses, farmers, and private landowners with small 4½ gallon casks known as 'Tommy Thumpers', delivered by their own horse and dray. The site was chosen because of its adequate supply of spring water. In 1880 James Forshaw died and the business was passed to Richard Forshaw and his aunt. During the miners' strike in 1893, Richard provided free bread and potatoes to hungry families. After the death of his father in 1930, Tom Forshaw continued the family business, gaining respect and admiration from employees and locals, being a knowledgeable farmer as well as a brewer. There was a Royal visit by Princess Margaret in 1987 to officially open the new kegging plant, marking the half stage of a £6 million expansion, including a new brewhouse.

Bradley Old Hall is one of the oldest buildings in Burtonwood, the original Hall having been built in the 14th century. The legends of secret passages and ghosts at the Hall are well known locally, enhanced by the Oaken Bed in the King's Room, a 7 ft long four-poster with measurements roughly carved in Roman numerals.

Coal mining played a great part in the lives of the families in the village from as far back as the 17th century. An entry in the chapel register dated 1697 records that a Moses Shaw was buried, described as a 'collier kild in pit'.

⌘ BYLEY-CUM-YATEHOUSE

Byley was first known as Biurley. Warren de Biurley who once owned an estate at Ravenscroft, took the name. The village lies three miles north of Middlewich and six miles south of Knutsford. It is bordered to the south by the river Dane and to the west by the Trent and Mersey Canal. It is a scattered area taking in the hamlets of Croxton, Ravenscroft, Yatehouse, Sublach and Leese.

Byley is an agricultural village – at one time the menfolk were mainly employed on the farms but as farming became more mechanised fewer farm hands were required and today the majority seek employment in Northwich, Middlewich or Holmes Chapel.

In the reign of Edward III the monks of Birkenhead owned an estate in the area and claimed manorial rights to use some of the properties as religious houses. With the Dissolution of the Monasteries the land was purchased from the Crown by Sir Geoffrey Shakerley. In 1846 Sir Walter Shakerley, a descendant of Sir Geoffrey, gave a plot of land to the village for the purpose of building a church; in 1847 the church was dedicated as St John the Evangelist, Byley-cum-Leese.

In the centre of the village on the main road stands the smithy. It was started over 200 years ago by Daniel Clark and entered its seventh generation of family blacksmiths before closing down. During the Second World War, an airfield was built at Byley. The site is now used by small industrial units and as warehousing.

⌘ CAPENHURST

Capenhurst is situated about six miles from Chester, and in the Domesday Book is mentioned as Capeles. At the time of the Domesday survey Capenhurst was owned by William FitzNigel of Halton.

In 1790 Richard Richardson purchased the manor and in 1792 built the new Hall. The old Hall, a lath and plaster building, was demolished but its site can still be traced near Dunkirk Lane and is marked 'Moat' on present day maps.

The church of the Holy Trinity, which is built of red sandstone believed to have been quarried in nearby Ledsham, was erected in 1858 by the Rev R. Richardson.

Over 40 men from Capenhurst and Ledsham served in the First World War and several were killed in action or died of wounds. In 1919–1920, as memorials to those who had given their lives for their country, six new bells were inserted in the tower in place of the previous four.

In the first hundred years of the church's history the names of Richardson and Maddock appear as churchwardens – one or other or both being in office. Indeed at one time there was a family of five Maddock brothers living in the village, whose ages ranged from 86 to 94, who were all, despite their ages, perfectly competent to manage their businesses.

The Capenhurst pinfold or pound is a square sandstone enclosure, believed to be the only one in Wirral. Animals were impounded for debts and kept at the owner's expense until redeemed.

In 1940, a wartime factory was built which became a branch of the United Kingdom Atomic Energy Authority. Capenhurst had been previously known as a dairy farming village, but it now had a fresh project in its midst. New inhabitants join in the village activities, but are frequently transferred to other places, so that the population in the village is frequently changing. The factory is now in the hands of British Nuclear Fuels Limited, who have a great interest in the village, helping in many ways, especially financially.

⌘ CAPESTHORNE & SIDDINGTON

Siddington is situated centrally five miles from Congleton, Holmes Chapel, Alderley Edge and Macclesfield. It is made up of scattered farms and cottages.

Redesmere Lake attracts both bird life and tourists and also yachtsmen to the sailing club. An unusual feature is the floating island which, to stop it straying, is anchored to the eastern edge of the lake.

Capesthorne is mentioned in the Domesday Book. The Hall has been owned by the Bromley-Davenport family since 1748. It is open to the public during the summer months.

The 15th century All Saints' church was built of a timber frame-work with wattle and daub filling. The weight of the heavy Kerridge flagstone roof caused the nave walls to bulge, so, in about 1815, they were strengthened by local red bricks, some being painted black and white to resemble the original timbers which remain underneath.

Following the closure of the school in July 1969, the building became the village hall and near the village pump are the plaques which have been awarded to Siddington in Cheshire's Best Kept Village competition.

Capesthorne Hall, home of the Bromley-Davenport family

⌘ CHELFORD

Chelford derives its name from Chellers Ford, where the stream crossed the road near the church.

Until 1774 the church was probably a wattle and daub building. In 1776 the present church of St John Evangelist was consecrated. Church registers date back to 1674. The name Abbey Farm witnesses that the parish church was served by the monks of the Abbey of St Werburgh at Chester prior to the Dissolution of the Monasteries.

The manor house is a fine building with its early Tudor black and white timber and plaster work but has many later additions. It boasts craftsmanship from Tudor, Stuart, Georgian and Victorian times.

When the railway arrived in 1842 the heart of the village was moved to a new location half a mile to the west. This new centre had a cattle market, village hall, and two public houses – the Dixon Arms and the Egerton Arms. The move occurred principally because the landowner of the Astle estate did not wish the line to cross his land.

The famous cattle market in Chelford was started by John Braggins in 1911 and joined by Frank Marshall in 1917 at the age of 14. It is a thriving and interesting market and one of international fame. Farmers, sellers and buyers come in from as far south as Cornwall to the north of Scotland and also from France and Holland.

There have been many changes in the village and its surroundings, with the reduction in the number of small farms resulting in larger units worked by fewer people. The sand quarry which provides much of the raw material for Pilkington Glass, is still very active today.

⌘ CHOLMONDELEY

Cholmondeley is situated in south Cheshire on the A49, halfway between Whitchurch and Tarporley. It is part of the estate owned by the Marquess of Cholmondeley. Most of its history is centred around the park and the ancient chapel owned by the Cholmondeley family. It is said that there are 24 ways of spelling Cholmondeley! It is of Saxon derivation, and was originally Calmunds Lea, ie a pasture meadow.

The younger son of a Marcher Baron of Malpas settled here in 1200; parts of the old house still stand. The family moved to the present castle in 1804.

The Old Hall suffered greatly during the Civil Wars and was almost destroyed in 1644. Many battles took place nearby. The Earl of Leinster who was there at the time, took many of his treasures and money packed in firkins to bury them at Bickley Hall. He died in 1659 and because of a dispute as to where he should be buried, his body lay in the Hall for a year. The treasures were found but not the

Cholmondeley Castle and park

money. Some years ago men out rabbiting unearthed some very old coins. The place where the money was buried is called the Money Pit.

The chapel is a splendid example of classical architecture built in 1716 by John Vanbrough. A chapel has stood on the site since the 13th century and permission to hold services there was given in 1323. Each marquess in turn has added to the chapel, which is now a cruciform shape and has a very beautiful screen and lovely east window of Flemish glass. The members of the family were buried at Malpas until the present burial ground was consecrated in 1920. The chapel and grounds are open to the public in the summer.

⌘ CHRISTLETON

The village of Christleton lies a little over two miles south-east of the city of Chester. The name means 'Christ's little town', which suggests an early Christian settlement.

The village featured largely in the Civil War, the battle of Rowton Moor being fought here in 1645, when the Parliamentarians' headquarters for the attack on Royalist Chester were at the Old Hall. The Royalists burned down the village and the only buildings which survived were the Old Hall, the church, the manor house, and part of the Glass House. The Trooper Inn took its name from the troopers of that war. The house known as The Old Farm was built immediately after the Civil War and bears the date 1653.

The Glass House was an inn for many years. It is here that the Beating of the Bounds begins and ends when this ancient ceremony takes place every ten years on Rogation Sunday. As the house is half in Christleton and half in Boughton, the rector and a host of parishioners, and their dogs, troop through it at the start of a 14 mile perambulation of the parish boundary, pausing in each of the five little townships which make up the parish of Christleton to pray for the farms, their workers, animals and crops.

The church of St James is the fourth to stand on its present site and, with the exception of the 15th century tower, was built in 1877.

The Shropshire Union Canal passes through Christleton and cargo-carrying narrow boats used to stop overnight, their horses being stabled at the Trooper. Now, in the summer, the boats come smartly decked out for holidays afloat.

'The Pit', overlooked by the picturesque black and white Dixon houses, was always a popular spot for feeding the ducks and, in the old hard winters, for skating. It was originally dug out as a marl pit and its clay was used to make the bricks for local buildings. Newcomers to the village soon learn not to call it 'the pond'.

The 'Roman' bridges are not really Roman at all, but three pretty little

'The Pit' at Christleton

medieval packhorse bridges. This is a favourite beauty spot with views of Beeston and Peckforton castles, the little river Gowy where children paddle and young people water their ponies, and the Hockenhull Platts nature reserve.

⌘ CHURCH MINSHULL

A picturesque, typically 17th century black and white Cheshire village, which may have evolved from the crossing of the river Weaver by a spur of the Roman road from Whitchurch to Middlewich.

The river Weaver at Church Minshull

There have been three churches on the same site and the present building, St Bartholomew's, completed in 1702, was partly financed by a local rate of 40 shillings in the pound and an appeal for Queen Anne's Bounty. A new three-arched bridge was built near the Weaver in 1698 because the old bridge had become too weak. Even this is now suffering from increasingly heavy traffic.

The mill, on one of two ancient sites, ground corn and provided electricity for the whole community until approximately 1960. Church Minshull was one of the last places to join the National Grid. Miss Billenge, the miller, in her later years a very eccentric character, kept the wheels turning although the lights often flickered if too much power was required all at once.

The canal which flows round the southern and eastern boundaries of the village is a branch of the Shropshire Union, and was once extensively used for transporting coal and salt. The Wharf House, with distinctive Dutch gables designed by Thomas Telford, was the loading point for a salt-packing business in the village, but now only private boats go by.

⌘ CLOTTON

Clotton is on a busy main road and was once a coaching stop on the route from London to Wales and to Parkgate. The latter, at the time, was the major port for the crossing to Ireland.

Close to the boundary with Duddon there is an outstanding example of a 'cop' (a hedge standing on top of a sandstone wall), forming an enclosure within which many 17th century clay pipes and pottery items were found, indicating occupation. Further examples of cops can be found throughout the village. To the south are examples and evidence of medieval field patterns.

By the 19th century there were many freeholders and two large landowners – Lord Tollemache and the Countess of Haddington. There was a National School in the village which was functioning between 1822 and 1873. The closure of the school followed the building of a new school in Duddon, though the old one still stands and is now a residential dwelling.

Today Clotton retains much of the character that prevailed over a hundred years ago with its farmhouses and dwellings, many of which have been painstakingly preserved by their owners. It is now in a conservation area. There are several examples of Cheshire's famous black and white houses in the village, such as Wynnstay House, Clotton Cottage and Townhouse Farm. There is also Georgian architecture, an example of which is Clotton Hall.

Agriculture is still important to Clotton though less so than it once was. An interesting point about the history of Clotton is the reversal of ownership of its lands. During its early history there were just a few large landowners, then in the 19th century there was a swing towards an increase in freeholder numbers. Now a reversal to this trend has come about as small farms are swallowed up by larger holdings.

⌘ CODDINGTON

Coddington in Roman times was said to have been quite an important staging post to Viroconium (Wroxeter). This was a distinct parish long before the Norman Conquest of 1066. The first church of Coddington was built when Christianity was established here in circa AD 655. Many of the church registers were destroyed in 1820 when a manservant of the rector set the rectory on fire. He was caught and taken prisoner as he was entering Chester with a stolen surplice in his possession, and was hanged for arson.

The mill is mentioned in the Domesday Book, the site probably in a small adjoining meadow. On the site of the present Mill House and orchard stood the village green where in Edward III's reign, Hawise, widow of Sir Ralph Botelier, claimed a market every Monday and a fair yearly on the eve and day of the Exaltation of the Holy Cross, 14th September.

In a field near the church, called the Mud Field, there is an artificial mound which may be an ancient tumulus, perhaps the 7th century burial place following a fight between the Mercians and the Britons (Welsh) in the days of Penda, King of Mercia.

Now Coddington is a hardworking farming community and is very much a tranquil backwater. Even the ducks who frequent the village pond are so 'laid back' they sleep in the road, oblivious to everyone!

⌘ COMBERBACH

Comberbach is situated in the parish of Great Budworth, which also includes Cogshall and Marbury. The village is still noted for the Spinner and Bergamot Inn, which is thought to have been named after two racehorses belonging to Smith-Barry of Marbury Hall. Soul caking was regularly performed here until the Second World War and the tradition was revived by present day villagers.

Cogshall or 'Cockshalle' (Coggs hyll in 1086) had a 14th century corn mill which was in use until 1880 but no longer exists.

Marbury Hall was privately owned until 1933 when it became a country club, having been largely rebuilt in 1843 in the French style. During the Second World War there was an army camp and a prisoner of war camp on the estate. Subsequently, the Hall was purchased by Imperial Chemical Industries, who housed their employees in the old barracks. It was completely demolished in the 1960s and now the site of the house and grounds has been developed into a country park by the Cheshire County Council.

On occasions Marbury Mere has been frozen over. One such event occurred in

1838, and two sheep were roasted on the ice; these were cut up and distributed with bread and rum to 4,000 people. There were two bands and the festivities continued into the next day. In the 1940s, many people were able to skate on the mere and one man drove across on a motor-bike and sidecar.

⌘ CUDDINGTON & SANDIWAY

Cuddington and Sandiway existed as separate villages from before Roman times and did not officially come together until 1935. Since then they have grown to form a large and thriving community. In the past the villages were very much involved with Vale Royal Abbey, the largest Cistercian settlement in England, begun in 1277.

The Wilbrahams moved to the area from Nantwich and built the beautiful Delamere Lodge, later known as Delamere House, on the fringe of the village. One Lady Wilbraham in the 19th century was known to ride around the village distributing red flannel, puddings and soups to the poor. The house was demolished in 1939 and the area used by the US Army during the Second World War. The 100 acre site has been developed and now forms a new community within Cuddington and Sandiway in the form of Delamere Park, a unique residential area.

A famous son of Cuddington and Sandiway must surely be the Victorian architect John Douglas. He was born in Norley Road and set up office in Chester in 1855. He built the imposing Gothic house Oakmere Hall, Sandiway Manor, now a delightful residential home, and of course the church dedicated to St John the Evangelist.

A four-legged character of much renown is *Blue Cap*, the foxhound who was entered for a speed trial in Newmarket in 1743 and won. So much was he revered that one of the local inns was renamed after him. A poem was also written in his honour. Quite a distinction for a foxhound.

A major event which had a great influence in the peaceful village was the coming of the railway. This was opened in July 1870 and the main line, Chester to Manchester, still operates. The branch line to Winsford now forms the peaceful walk known as the Whitegate Way.

⌘ CULCHETH

Culcheth's name first appears in Norman times. Medieval happenings included the building of Culcheth Hall, the family home of the lord of the manor. Later, in the Civil War, a Protestant neighbour won a victory for the Roundheads near the present Raven Inn. This was Lieutenant-Colonel John Holcroft, whose daughter Maria married the most notorious local character, Colonel Blood, who nearly stole the Crown Jewels in 1671.

The building of the Liverpool to Manchester railway coincided with a scandalous number of illegitimate births in the village. This must have helped to produce the total population of 2,091, which was entered in the 1841 census.

Now Culcheth has around 8,000 people. In 1974 it finally became part of Warrington after being part of Leigh, then of Golborne. Since 1946 Atomic Energy has created many jobs in Culcheth and at nearby Risley. Warrington, Manchester and the Wigan area are other centres of employment and there is a plastics factory in the village.

Newchurch parish church, which gave its name to part of Culcheth, began as a Tudor chapel of ease for Winwick church, although the Catholic Culcheth squires ignored it and had their own chapel. The fire at the old church in 1903 caused great excitement. A passing train driver helped to raise the alarm with his locomotive's whistle. Sadly the horsedrawn fire engine was too late, but a new building was ready by 1904.

⌘ DARESBURY

Daresbury lies to the south of Warrington, a peaceful village built along part of the old Roman road, but now bypassed by the main road to Chester. Daresbury was, and still is to some extent, a farming community, although most of the farms are

The Lewis Carroll memorial window in Daresbury church

34

now in the nearby hamlet of Newton-by-Daresbury, separated from the village by the M56 motorway.

Newton Cross once stood hundreds of years ago on the common land. It was believed that if the stones from the cross were removed a curse would fall upon the farms and all the farm animals would perish. As long ago as the early 18th century, even though the cross had been reduced to a few large stone blocks, this fear still existed and rather than disturb the stones the farmer would plough around them. This 'curse' was eventually lifted when the construction of the motorway necessitated the temporary removal of the stones.

Newton-by-Daresbury was the birthplace of Charles Lutwidge Dodgson, better known as Lewis Carroll, the author of *Alice in Wonderland*. He was born in 1832 at the parsonage in Morphany Lane, son of the parson of Daresbury. The building, on the glebe land one and a half miles from the village, was burned down in 1883 and today the site is commemorated by a stone plinth along the roadside.

Although there was a church in the village as long ago as 1159 the present church was restored in 1872, though the tower dates from 1550. In 1934 a stained glass memorial window was dedicated to celebrate the centenary of Lewis Carroll's birth.

Each year at the beginning of September the village held the Hatton Show, the only village show in Cheshire still under canvas. The show was in existence in 1894 and was originally held in the nearby village of Hatton but since the Second World War has been held in Daresbury.

⌘ DARNHALL

Of the local hostelries, the Raven Inn has connections with William Corbett, a 19th century occupant of Darnhall Hall, whilst at Wettenhall are to be found the Boot and Slipper, formerly the Royal Oak, and the Little Man of Wettenhall.

Darnhall itself boasts a mill, dating back to 1829, which with its twin water-wheels was fully operational until 1970, and a school, the charter of which goes back to 1662 when Elizabeth Venables, wife of the commander of the land forces that captured Jamaica for the British, left £220 in her will to her son to employ a schoolmaster or mistress to educate the people of Darnhall.

Darnhall is of the 'Vale Royal' where Edward I, the first English Earl of Chester, in thanksgiving for his life having been spared from shipwreck and drowning, fulfilled a vow to build an abbey for 100 white-robed black-cloaked monks of the Cistercian order. Started in 1266 as Darnhall Abbey, the monastery moved to Vale Royal after a few years and thereafter the manor of Darnhall was the scene of much strife between peasants and Church. Indeed the severed head of one luckless inhabitant, John de Boddeworth, was used as a football by his executioners.

Nearer the present day, the final occupants of the Hall from the end of the 19th century were the Verdin family, proprietors of the largest salt works in the area, landowners, philanthropists and general benefactors who at one time had 4,000 acres of Darnhall countryside in title. Sir Richard Verdin, the last occupant, died in the 1970s; villagers were invited to his 21st birthday celebrations and recognised their debt, and indeed that of Winsford, to the beneficence of his family.

On the site of a Second World War searchlight battery, an extra-terrestrial satellite telescope controlled from Jodrell Bank receives messages from a world that was old long before W. H. Verdin planted the magnificent avenue of horse chestnuts lining the route to the Hall.

⌘ DAVENHAM

Tradition says that Davenham was a place of worship in remote ages before the Christian era. The Celts are said to have practised their religious rites here and there is also a tradition that later, St Wilfrid established a church here during his journeys through Cheshire.

On the Davenham road at one time there could be seen three large stones, one in Hartford Road, one in Church Street and one on Shipbrook Hill. These are believed to have been used as markers in planning roads.

St Wilfrid's church, Davenham

The first recorded mention of Davenham is in the Domesday Book, where it is called Deveneham. Most of the land in Davenham eventually became the property of John Hoskin Harper, who was the chief landowner during the middle of the 19th century. A memorial erected to his memory can still be seen at the junction of London Road and Fountain Lane.

The Norman church was replaced in 1680 and a spire was erected. In 1841 reconstruction of the present church of St Wilfrid was begun; the church was lengthened, the nave and the aisles widened, the north and south transepts, organ chamber and vestries added. The spire has twice been struck by lightning, in 1850 and again during the 1980s.

⌘ DEAN ROW

A signpost off the busy A34 road at Handforth points to Dean Row. The village is bounded at one side by the river Bollin, a name used by the Wilmslow family of Le Boleyn.

Dean Row chapel, built about 1693, which was originally Presbyterian and later became Unitarian, is said to be the oldest Nonconformist place of worship in the county of Cheshire. The grounds are entered through a lychgate, the chapel being scheduled as an ancient monument. Nearby a Methodist chapel, opened in 1849, now houses a firm of instrument makers. It is said that when the choir and musicians went carol singing in 1887 the night was not without adventure, since one fell into the river, another slipped into a pump trough and yet another knocked a spigot out of a water butt, releasing floods of water over the singers' feet! Let us hope they raised a lot of money for their new hymn books.

A school built in 1861 was sometimes hard put to make ends meet because local farmers employed their children as labourers at busy times and school levies were not paid. The adjoining school house was occupied by the minister of the Unitarian chapel until it and the school building were sold to be converted to a private home named 'Chapel Grange'.

Old customs included 'boon day', when the locals gave a day's work to help a new tenant farmer. Ploughing matches also took place, and 'Riding Stang', which was beating on tins outside the house of any man who ill-treated his wife.

⌘ DELAMERE

Although there is a very beautiful parish church of St Peter, local buildings are so scattered that Delamere tends to be thought of as a district rather than a village.

Having the forest on the doorstep is Delamere's main claim to fame. Once Delamere was full of game and in the days when Sir John Done entertained King James I, 'deer both red and fallow and fish and fowl in the meres abounded'. As well as deer in the forest, wolves, boars and foxes roamed.

Hatchmere Lake in Delamere Forest

Oakmere is the largest lake in Delamere and Mary Ann Hollingworth, 'the old woman of Oakmere', lived on the shore of the mere in a cottage made from a whale's ribs. She arrived one day in a donkey cart and was given permission to settle there. The year was 1815, superstition was rampant and wild stories of every kind were circulated about her. The truth appears to be that she was an English woman who had married a German and gone to reside in Hanover. Her husband having subsequently died, she returned home and was waiting to be joined by her son.

Watching the road for him one evening, she saw a man approaching whom she assumed to be her son. He stopped at a nearby cottage to speak to someone there and the mother hurried inside to prepare a meal for him, but although she waited until darkness fell, he did not appear. Next morning, gazing anxiously across the lake, she saw men carrying a sack which they dumped in the water. Alarmed that something dreadful had befallen her son, she persuaded the authorities to investigate, and sure enough, the sack was found to contain the body of a man. But not her son's body; he arrived next day!

⌘ DODLESTON

Dodleston village is just five miles from Chester, at the foot of the Welsh hills. It is mentioned in the Domesday Book of 1086 at a value of 40 shillings. The castle served as a watchtower on the Welsh border but only the mound remains by the churchyard today.

The church of St Mary was endowed by Edgar, King of Mercia in AD 980 and the village celebrated a millennium of worship with a flower festival. On Sunday mornings the church bells ring out as they have done since pre-Reformation times.

There has always been a strong connection with the Grosvenor family and the village has many cottages built for the estate workers. They have the date and a 'W' (for Westminster) in the brickwork, but no front doors. This, it is said, is because when the agent of the estate knocked on the door he was always told to 'Come round the back' – so no more front doors were put into estate cottages.

During the Second World War the chapel was used as the headquarters of the Home Guard – one member put a bullet through the roof while cleaning his gun! They used to drill in the school yard and their proudest moment was when an enemy plane came down nearby and they stood guard over it.

As in all communities characters abound. The church choir was one of the best around but there were some members who wouldn't sing when the wind was in the north. Another villager refused to milk the cows on his billiards day. Then there was the doctor's surgery, held in a rented room, where the consultations were hardly private as the spinsters who owned it used to listen in!

⌘ DUTTON

Dutton, recorded in the Domesday Book as Duntune, has always been and still is a farming village. Although there is no village centre, not even a church, Dutton has much to commend it.

The river Weaver flows through the meadows, and in 1735 the first lock was constructed at Dutton. The present lock was rebuilt in the middle of the 19th century and Dutton Locks was at one time a very busy place coping with boats carrying salt, and later ICI chemicals, to Liverpool. Nowadays the river traffic is mainly pleasure craft.

The Trent and Mersey Canal, opened in 1777, meanders through the fields. One of the main cargoes on this stretch of water was china clay. This was brought from Cornwall to Runcorn and then carried by narrow boats to the Potteries. Manufactured china goods for export were brought back on the return journey. The canal tunnel which connects Dutton with Preston Brook is one of the longest in the country.

With the coming of the railways a viaduct was built to span the Weaver valley. Work commenced in 1834 and the 22 elegant sandstone arches, which rest on cotton wool to assist resilience, took over ten years to build.

In the reign of King John, Hugh de Dutton, who lived at Dutton Hall, was given the 'minstrilsie' of Cheshire. This meant that all musicians in Cheshire had to pay him and his successive heirs an annual licence fee for the privilege of playing their instruments. These proceedings, held at Chester, always ended with the proclamation 'God bless the King and the Heir of Dutton'! in 1934 Dutton Hall, a beautiful magpie building, was bought by Dewars the whisky family, dismantled brick by brick and rebuilt in Sussex.

⌘ EATON (TARPORLEY)

A small friendly village where traditional black and white thatched cottages nestle side by side with modern houses. It is set in a pleasant situation below the hill where once a Bronze Age hunter left his axe head, where a wealthy Roman built his country villa and where, in the Middle Ages, a hall with double moat was occupied by the lord of the manor.

An abundance of wells and streams served the inhabitants with water until the late 1930s, the Anglo-Saxon name 'Eaton' meaning a settlement or village by water.

In the middle of the village is the post office, which has been in the same family's hands since stamps were first issued. And also in the centre of the village, where tradition has it that a medieval preaching cross once stood, a new cross to commemorate the Queen's Jubilee was erected in 1977 on the old steps.

Education in Eaton started in dame schools in cottages, and then in 1806 Thomas Hough built the first school. He supported it at his own expense and left £1,000 in his will to continue this support. A new school was built in the 1960s and the old school and school house have been divided into two houses. An open book still decorates the doorway of the school house with the inscription,

> 'God is Truth, The Word is Truth
> The Spirit is Truth, and Love is Truth'

The village hall, The Jessie Hughes Institute, was built in 1926 and named after the wife of the then Tarporley rector.

⌘ FARNDON

Farndon, which is mentioned in the Domesday Book as Ferendon, lies on a Roman road and it is very likely that there was a ford or ferry here from Roman times until the bridge was built. The first bridge was probably made of wood and was replaced by one of stone in 1345.

There is a legend that two Welsh princes were thrown over the bridge and drowned. It is said their ghosts can be seen and screams heard on dark nights.

During the 7th century, Chad, Bishop of Lichfield, visited the area, which was part of the Diocese of Lichfield at that time; consequently the church was dedicated to St Chad. Part of the church was destroyed by fire and rebuilt in the 1658. The Barnston chapel contains a unique window called the Armorial Window, showing

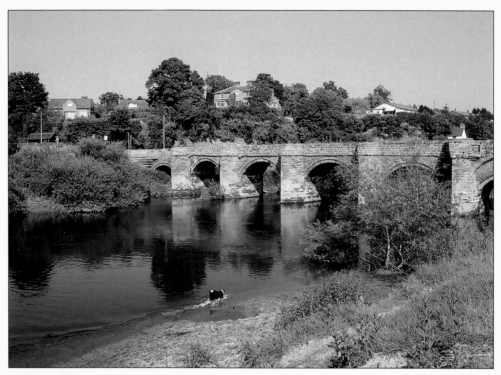

Bridge over the river Dee at Farndon

the arms of the Gamul, Mainwaring and Barnston families, who were all involved in the Civil War.

At one time, the church floor was covered with rushes renewed each year. Today, at Rushbearing, the graves are all dressed with flowers.

In AD 924 King Edward the Elder died at Farndon after dealing with a revolt. His body was taken to Winchester for burial.

John Speed, a famous son of Farndon, was born in the village in 1542. He was a tailor by trade, but later became a renowned cartographer and historian. Later in life, he moved to London with his family; it is reported that he had 18 children. He worked in London until his death in 1629 and he is buried in St Giles, Cripplegate, London.

Strawberry growing was, for many years, the main occupation of Farndon, but never quite recovered after the Second World War, when much of the land had to be ploughed up to provide grain. During the 1920s and 1930s, men and women used to flock into the village to pick the strawberries; they were known as 'Dodgers' and were accommodated in huts provided by the growers.

⌘ FRODSHAM

Overton Hill is an outstanding landmark formed over a million years ago of red, brown and yellow sandstone, rising to 365 ft with a panoramic view overlooking the village to the Mersey estuary, sweeping round to the Welsh hills. In 1865 some enterprising person built the Mersey View pavilion and pleasure grounds on the summit, with swing-boats and donkey rides.

The parish church of St Lawrence was built in the 12th century on the site of a previous Saxon church. The interior was once described by visiting historians as a 'magnificent little cathedral' – the belfry is comfortably furnished for the ringers of the eight bells.

Frodsham is a small community of 8,000 residents. There are two main thoroughfares – Main Street, which boasts being one of the widest roads in England, and Church Street. Each Thursday a market is held in Main Street, the origins of which go back to the 13th century.

In medieval times Frodsham was a thriving port with salt coming from mid-Cheshire by packhorses, then by river to Liverpool and beyond. Cheshire cheese was also exported and a warehouse was built on the river bank to accommodate this.

In Main Street are a number of 17th century timber-framed cottages, some still retaining their thatched roofs. The oldest surviving cottages, possibly built in the 14th century, stand on The Rock on the original road through the village. The Georgian houses remain in all their glory, little altered from the time of being built.

Frodsham Marshes, which lie to the west between the M56 and the Manchester Ship Canal, are of great importance to ornithologists, with nearly 200 different species of birds recorded.

⌘ GAWSWORTH

The parish of Gawsworth is set in a beautiful part of Cheshire, between the hills at the eastern edge of the county and the flat land of the Cheshire Plain. It is named as Goursourde in the Domesday survey of 1086, and there were settlements here in Neolithic and Bronze Age times.

The Hall and church are probably on the site of an old wooden chapel and stone manor house where the de Orreby family lived when they were granted the manor of Gawsworth for 'one caparisoned horse'. The Fittons, who owned the manor for 400 years, rebuilt the Hall, the church, and the old rectory, and landscaped the surrounding area. The part immediately round the Hall is surrounded by a long wall dating from Tudor times and includes a medieval tilting ground.

The tombs and effigies of four generations of the Fitton family are to be seen in the attractive sandstone 15th century church of St James with its eight-pinnacled tower, winged dragon gargoyles, and armorial bearings. It was restored in the

Gawsworth's Old Rectory

19th century. Mary Fitton, daughter of Sir Edward Fitton, is said by some authors to be the Dark Lady of Shakespeare's sonnets.

Another Gawsworth character was Samuel 'Maggotty' Johnson, last of the paid English jesters, also known as Lord Flame after a character in a play he wrote and performed in at the Haymarket theatre in London. His ghost is said to haunt the village, riding on a white horse. He is buried in 'Maggotty's Wood', now owned by the National Trust.

It is pleasant to stroll round the village and see the interesting buildings – Gawsworth Court, the gate house with its 20 inch thick walls; the rectory; the New Hall, begun by Lord Mohun; the Old Post Office – the oldest shop in Gawsworth, in the same family for three generations; the White House, formerly the village school; and the Harrington Arms – a Queen Anne building, with its cobbled forecourt, farm at the rear, and old oak bar. At the other end of the parish is the only other inn – the Rising Sun.

⌘ GOOSTREY

The history of Goostrey can be traced back to Saxon times. St Luke's church is a dominant part of the village and one of the few remaining churches with a moat, albeit without water.

Jodrell Bank, Goostrey, at night

Legend, backed by old church accounts books, says that the huge yew tree outside the church door provided arrows for the Cheshire bowmen, and in 1365 records show that land was granted to two archers for distinguished conduct at the battle of Poitiers.

The showing of gooseberries is a celebrated custom of the area. To take part you must be an accredited member of the society and be prepared to have your berries examined during the growing period, even though you would never dream of cheating! It is a serious business when the catchweights and pennyweights come out on show day, but a wonderful feeling when you are declared champion.

In 1956 in a field on the northern side of Goostrey, Professor Bernard Lovell was responsible for the setting up of Jodrell Bank, at that time the world's largest radio telescope. Known locally as Lovell's Saucer, the landmark can be seen from most parts of Cheshire. In the exhibition centre, pieces of rock brought back from man's first landing on the moon, one of the space suits and samples of space age technology are on view to the public, whilst the planetarium offers an insight to the heavens. In the grounds of Jodrell Bank stands the arboretum belonging to the Botany Department of Manchester University – old and new sciences side by side.

⌘ GRAPPENHALL

Both old and new buildings combine to make up the village, which has a seven and a half mile boundary. In 1977 the ancient custom of beating the bounds was revived after a gap of 56 years.

The old part of the village is entered by two hump-backed bridges over the Bridgewater Canal and the street between them is known as Church Street. This

Grappenhall village and St Wilfrid's church

for the most part is still cobbled, and one feels on entering the village, that one has stepped back in time. The sandstone-built Ram's Head, with an old sun-dial on the wall, and the cream-washed Parr Arms with its hanging baskets and coat of arms over the door, and the stocks just outside, all help to keep this illusion.

The church of St Wilfrid dates back to the 12th century and is built of sandstone, which came from a local quarry. It makes a very impressive feature and is surrounded by an interesting graveyard.

The village school was built in 1846. Its playing field extends to the Bridgewater Canal, which is cut in a loop around the village thus making it free from heavy traffic. During the summer months narrow boats of all lengths and assorted cabin cruisers pass through the village or are moored along the towpath. The towpaths are kept in good repair and offer some lovely walks, linking with footpaths and lanes through this part of the county.

There are still some of the original buildings associated with the cutting of the canal in 1759–65, including a small grain warehouse or store for local farmers who made use of this new mode of transport. This is now a private house, as is a grander house built for an official to oversee this section of the canal as it was built.

⌘ GREAT BUDWORTH

Argued by some to be one of Cheshire's loveliest villages, Great Budworth, or the village on the hill, lies three miles north of Northwich and eight miles south of Warrington, overlooking Budworth Mere. Its name derives from Saxon times, meaning Budda's enclosure.

Its character results from the variety of buildings, including the square-framed cottages, closely packed on either side of the main High Street. Because of this very original and charming setting the village is a popular location for films and television dramas.

Before the arrival of mains water in 1934 the village obtained its water from a pump at the bottom of High Street. This was later enclosed by a pumphouse, built in 1869 by Rowland Eyles Egerton Warburton, composer of the verse inscribed above the pump. He was known as the 'Rhyming Poet of Arley' and wrote verses which can still be found today on nearby houses, signposts and in the George and Dragon porch.

Industries which flourished in the 19th century included brickmaking, saddlery, shoemaking, and clock-case making in Clock Cottages.

A wake to commemorate the dedication of the church of St Mary and All Saints is still observed on the old date of 11th November. The custom of eating flummery, or furmenty, a mixture of boiled wheat, milk, sugar and spice, was observed in some households on Wakes Sunday. Today villagers are entertained by nearby Comberbach Mummers performing the local soul caking play. This is based on an ancient ritual with Death and Resurrection as its theme. Characters include the

Looking over Budworth Mere to Great Budworth

'Letter-in', Quack Doctor, Dairy Dout and Beelzebub. A real skull with bones strung together is used for 'The Horse', which enables the mouth to open and the teeth to snap.

⌘ HALTON

The residents of Halton village thought they would be completely swamped during the 1960s by the joining together of the twin towns of Runcorn and Widnes to form the new Borough of Halton. However, the village has managed to retain much of its identity. Main Street, which leads to the castle, is almost unchanged.

The present St Mary's church, just below the castle, replaced the original in 1820; the stone vicarage was built around 1650, and the recently restored library building in 1773, which is now used as a village hall.

Mention must be made of nearby Norton Priory, which was built by Augustinian friars in 1155, but at the Dissolution of the Monasteries was purchased from the Crown by Sir Richard Brooke. The family had close ties with Halton, where they were regarded lords of the manor. Early in the 20th century the family left and the house fell into decay. It was demolished in the 1930s, except for the crypt and a wall with a statue of St Christopher. These have been incorporated

Norton Priory, near Halton

into an informative museum, with the grounds displaying the finds of an
archaeological dig with many interesting remains.

⌘ HELSBY

Helsby's history goes back 2,000 years, when Iron Age tribesmen – probably of the
Cornovii tribe – constructed a hill fort on top of Helsby Tor (464 ft high), a
northern frontier post of their tribal territory. Helsby itself was built at the foot of
the hill above the level of the undrained marshland.

In medieval times, the great Forest of Delamere reached as far as Helsby and
beyond. The marshes which stretch northwards to the river Mersey, where the
early inhabitants kept their cattle, are now more extensively drained than hitherto
and turned into agricultural land. The M56 motorway was built on this land in
1971.

The rocky escarpments on the hill have a strong resemblance to a man's face.
This part of the hill is a favourite haunt of rock climbers and is a recognised
training place. Guide books quote, 'As long as Helsby wears a hood, the weather's
never very good'.

In the latter part of the 18th century the mail was carried on horseback through
Helsby. In 1795 the postboy was stopped and his mail bags stolen by a man named

From Helsby Tor, looking over the Mersey Plain towards Ince

Lowndes. Three years later Lowndes was seen and identified in Exeter and brought to Chester for trial. He was convicted and sentenced to death, his body to be gibbeted on Helsby Hill.

⌘ HENBURY & BROKEN CROSS

Henbury, three miles from Macclesfield, is a fascinating village, mentioned in the Domesday Book. It was known as Henbury in 1383 though the name has varied frequently through the centuries. However, without its neighbouring village of Broken Cross, Henbury would by now almost certainly have lost its identity.

Broken Cross village, with its assortment of small shops and its clock of considerable age, has been at the centre of a very busy crossroads for over a thousand years. It is thought that at one time there may have been a cross in the village centre, or perhaps its name arose from the nature of the crossroads, which did not form a regular intersection, though now they are joined by a modern roundabout. Here on the turnpike road from Macclesfield to Knutsford, crossed by the older salters' route, stood the toll house. Money, fraudulently minted in the village by a coining gang, is thought to have been passed on here.

The church of St Thomas, built in 1844 as a daughter church of Prestbury, was only licensed for marriages in 1870 when the local squire's daughter was married. It is beautified by the engraved glass doors in memory of Sir Vincent de Ferranti of Henbury Hall, founder of the electronics firm. The slender broach spire can be seen from quite a distance across the fields.

An elderly resident remembered his mother relating how she and other women sat on stones in a circle making bricks at Brickbank Farm. Here, in 1971, when a field was ploughed some large stones were discovered. Later excavation revealed the remains of a stone circle measuring six metres in diameter. The circle had an alignment with the mid-winter rising sun. Could these brickworkers have been unwittingly using a prehistoric site as their work place?

The Plague Stone, originally in a rather unpleasant spot known as Sugar Pit Dump, has now been moved nearer to a gate leading to the Hall. Legend has it that the stone used to turn over at midnight! The grey squirrel was first successfully introduced to Britain in Henbury Park as a game animal, but little thought seems to have been given to the damage it might cause in years ahead.

⌘ HIGH LEGH

High Legh stands 240 ft above sea level, on the escarpment overlooking the Mersey, midway between Knutsford and Warrington.

During the reign of Henry II, the manor was rented in two parts, to two families, who assumed the local name. They became known as *Legh* of East Hall, and *Leigh* of West Hall. Each family had its own chapel, both of which are still in existence, one of them being now the parish church of St John, and the other St Mary's, the private chapel of the Cornwall Legh family. In 1912 the Leighs of West Hall sold out to the Leghs of East Hall. Both Halls were taken over by the army in the Second World War, and were demolished in 1962. When the army moved into the Hall, the Cornwall Legh family moved to High Legh House. The name Cornwall was added in 1730, when George Legh married Anna Maria, daughter and heiress of Francis Cornwall, Baron of Burford.

St Mary's chapel is probably the oldest building in the village, dating from 1581, and it may have replaced a chapel mentioned in the Domesday Book. Built of sandstone, it contains some fine carved oak. The parish church of St John, an attractive black and white building, was originally the West Hall private chapel. It is the third building on this site, and was built in 1893.

The Independent Methodist chapel in Northwood Lane, was once a gamekeeper's cottage. The movement was started in High Legh in 1783, by Betty O'Kell. The Congregation met in her farmhouse kitchen, and was known for many years as 'O'Kells Meeting'.

⌘ HOLMES CHAPEL

Holmes Chapel, or Church Hulme, was originally just called Hulme. It has come a long way since it was merely a church and a few cottages in the middle of a wood.

A fire on 10th July 1753, burned down 18 of the 20 houses; only the church, the two cottages behind and the Red Lion escaped. Even the lime trees in the churchyard were scorched.

St Luke's church is the product of many centuries. It was originally half-timbered, later having brick walls added. In 1705 the church was extended and three plaster ceilings were constructed. Then in 1935, due to the need for repair, the ceilings were removed revealing the beautiful timber in all its glory.

The Methodist chapel on Knutsford Road was built in 1900. John Wesley on a journey with two friends from Oxford to Manchester, on 16th March 1738, preached to the customers of the Red Lion.

Thomas Hall from Cranage bought the Hermitage in 1702 and was a great benefactor to the village. He built the bridge over the Dane down Coach Lane, now Hermitage Lane, also a cottage on Macclesfield Road. Romper Lowe lived in the cottage, and was notorious for smuggling salt across the river Dane to avoid taxes, hence the name Saltersford. It is said that the salt was forded across in coffins.

Saltersford Hall was built in the late 18th century, and was owned by the Toler family. It has had various uses through the years, being a reformatory, approved school for boys, agricultural college and a Home Office school.

Grannie Mandeville started the first May Day celebrations in 1879 and Miss Elizabeth Mandeville was the first May Day Queen to be crowned. The present-day Mandevilles still run the bakery on Macclesfield Road. Old Mr W. Mandeville baked a 'Fertility Bread' which was eaten far and wide, and Dr Lionel Picton recommended it to all infertile ladies; the success rate was apparently very good!

⌘ INCE

Ince is a small Cheshire parish whose boundaries comprise seven miles of water and a mile and a half of land. An old-world village, its known history began when St Werburgh's remains were brought to Chester in the 10th century. The small

The night-time view towards Ince from Runcorn

community which was founded to serve her shrine was endowed with several granges, Ince being one. The Benedictines who took over Chester, took over Ince, and the remains of their priory are here to be seen. The long 14th-century chancel of St James' church dates from monastic use. After the Dissolution of the Monasteries, Chester Cathedral continued to pay £4 6s 8d a year to the vicar of Ince until the 20th century.

The building of the railway made the centuries-old ferry redundant. The Ship Canal built through the parish made access to the Mersey for shrimp fishing (a staple but unreliable and uncomfortable industry) difficult and industrial growth gave more stable jobs to the men of Ince. In the last few decades of the 20th century the Stanlow refinery has extended across the marshes right into the parish. The site of Ince Hall with its once beautiful gardens is now occupied by oil tanks. On the Frodsham side there are the Ince power stations and Shellstar, and over 400 acres owned by Shell, destined for more industry.

The village remains a quiet oasis of peace surrounded by industry. It still has an outlook on river and mountain, wood and plain; and the church has a simple charm and an atmosphere of prayer that endears it to those who love simple places and simple things.

⌘ KELSALL

Nestling beneath the sandstone ridge which runs across Cheshire from Helsby to Beeston, Kelsall has been home for many settlers. There are remains of an Iron Age fort on Kelsborrow Hill, one of a number of hill forts on the track linking Wales to the Pennines. Indeed, Kelsall's past and present development is closely linked with roads. The Roman Watling Street passed through Kelsall en route to the salt towns where salt was collected to pay the wages (salarium) of the garrison at Deva (Chester).

There are not many very old houses in Kelsall, probably because of a fire which destroyed most of the village in 1738. However, there is an old farmhouse in Frodsham Street, thought to be 17th century and a thatched cottage, thought to be 16th century, in Green Lane. The old 18th century gaol opposite the Royal Oak which was obviously built before the days of prison reform, has been preserved.

Kelsall's chalybeate (mineral) springs are frequently mentioned in books about Cheshire and have a reputation for promoting good health and longevity – many residents reaching 90 years or more. However, the lady who fell down a well, and is reputed to haunt Old Coach Road may not have agreed!

In contrast to Kelsall's rapid growth, Willington, Kelsall's nearest neighbour, has remained predominantly rural. The scenic valley known locally as 'Little Switzerland' leads down to the attractively situated Boot Inn. Off Chapel Lane there is a row of almshouses built by the Tomkinson family of Willington Hall. The Hall itself was built in 1829 and is a handsome brick mansion in an Elizabethan style, standing in impressive grounds.

⌘ KETTLESHULME

The name, Kettleshulme, was first recorded in 1285 but it probably has Viking origins. The area must have been well known in Saxon times, as evidenced by the Bow Stones which are thought to have Saxon religious connections. The Salt Way from Nantwich and Middlewich through to Sheffield and Chesterfield brought travellers over Reed Bridge and along Flatts Lane. Kettleshulme continues to be the hub of footpaths in every direction and attracts a stream of ramblers throughout the year, as well as young climbers bound for Windgather Rocks.

Until 1921 Kettleshulme was in the parish of Prestbury but, following boundary changes, became part of the parish of Taxal with Kettleshulme.

Originally it was St John's church at Saltersford that cared for worshippers. Taxal church, however, provides much of the evidence that we have of early history and property. It holds the record of the Thomas Ouffe Charity which has helped the poor since 1628, particularly benefiting apprentices and students to this day.

From the 18th century Methodism had a large following in the valley and, for many years, Methodist preachers gathered at Pym Chair, in the open air, and attracted large congregations.

Both silk and cotton were woven in the local cottages and around 1797 William

Windgather Rocks, near Kettleshulme

Brocklehurst of Gap House erected a two-storey building alongside the Todd Brook at Lumb Hole, to be used as weaving rooms.

The prize for the oddest fellow in village history would still be awarded to Amos Broadhurst of Priest Farm, whose beard grew to 10 ft long and was proudly displayed on special occasions!

⌘ KINGSLEY

This 'much sought after' village lies in the north of the county and extends from the river Weaver to Delamere Forest. Ancient in origin, dating back to Saxon times, it is a rich source of material for local historians. Old mansions and manor houses – Kingsley Hall, Crewood Hall, Peel Hall and Catten Hall – still enhance the village, having been demolished and rebuilt over the centuries, whilst Kingsley Mill is still a going concern, carrying on a tradition started in pre-Norman days.

Throughout the ages the villagers of Kingsley have had a reputation for independence, as exemplified by their staunch Parliamentarianism during the Civil War and in matters of religion, by early institution of a Quaker meeting house, a Baptist chapel and Methodist chapels. The Quaker meeting house was built along with a burial ground as early as 1686. It is now a private residence. The Baptists had a chapel in Chapel Lane but this has now vanished without trace. There have been various Methodist chapels over the years; the first was built in 1787.

The parish church of St John the Evangelist was consecrated in 1851. The tower, with its clock, dominates the approach to the village from Frodsham, whilst across the road lies the cemetery with the Kingsley and Newton war memorial.

The number of shops has declined since the Second World War as improving transport has enabled villagers to make their purchases further afield, but the atmosphere of the village remains. The two hostelries – the Horseshoe and the Red Bull – are long established, the latter dating from 1771.

⌘ LINDOW & ROW OF TREES

Whoever had heard of the parish of Lindow before the discovery in 1984 in nearby Lindow Moss of the body of a Celtic Iron Age man, well preserved in a peat bog? Lindow Man, or 'Lindow Pete' as the popular newspapers nicknamed him, now resides in the British Museum, and the riddle of his death will probably remain a mystery forever. He certainly met with a violent end – killed by blows to the head, then garrotted, and finally sacrificed to the bog.

Although entirely surrounded now by other villages and hamlets (Alderley Edge, Chorley, Row of Trees) and joined to the town of Wilmslow by roads and buildings which have developed over the years, the present parish of Lindow still maintains all the features of an English village.

The hamlet of Row of Trees is attached to Lindow although in the parish of Chorley. Thirty lime trees were planted here in the 17th century, and there are many conflicting stories told of their origin. The original trees have since decayed, but during the 20th century were replanted. One story says they were planted as a guide to travellers, to keep them out of the treacherous Lindow Bog. Whatever the origin, they are a focal point for the village.

Row of Trees has many buildings of note. Row of Trees Farm, a lovely black and white building, was built in 1603. In 1665 a lady visited the farm to escape from the Great Plague in London. Alas, she was already a victim of this disease, so she was isolated in an adjoining barn, and fed from the end of a hayfork. She succumbed to the dreaded illness and was buried in a nearby field. A stone inscribed E.S. 1665 was placed over the spot, and can still be seen today.

⌘ LITTLE BUDWORTH

Little Budworth lies midway between Winsford and Tarporley and was mentioned in the Domesday Book, where it was called Bodeurde.

The area was extensively wooded in earlier times and was part of the great forests of Mara and Mondrum which covered the centre of Cheshire in the Middle Ages. Little Budworth Common is designated as a Site of Special Scientific Interest.

For centuries the Egertons lived at Oulton Park, providing employment on

Oulton Park, Little Budworth

their estate for local people and playing a beneficent role in village life. In the 18th century there was a dame school founded by the Egerton family, who wished to express their gratitude to a small boy, 'Irish' Jack Gawley, who kept them supplied with food during an outbreak of the plague, no other villager being brave enough to approach the Hall.

There have been other benefactors in Little Budworth's history. The almshouses at the west end of the village stand testament to the generosity of Dame Isabella Dodds and Ralph Kirkham who bequeathed money to help the poor and needy. Three charities currently provide funds for the maintenance of the almshouses.

Village folk are still involved in agriculture and there are a few farms and cottages, part of the Oulton estate, but many newcomers commute to the city each day, returning thankfully down leafy lanes frothing with cow parsley in summer, glistening with blackberries in the autumn and occasionally blocked by drifting snow in the winter.

Many seek out the village for the race track, which uses roads that American forces built when stationed in the park during the Second World War.

⌘ LITTLE SUTTON

Before the Conquest Little Sutton belonged to the secular canons of St Werburgh and passed to their successors the Benedictine monks, who held the land until the Dissolution of the Monasteries. It is believed that the monks planted the fine yew hedge that can be seen in Ledsham Road.

The historian Ormerod records that in 1811 an underground burial chamber was discovered south of the former Hall. This, he believed, was a cemetery belonging to the secular canons. The present Sutton Hall, an attractive Georgian building, was built in the latter part of the 18th century and was the home of the White family for many years.

A ghostly resident of Little Sutton gives his name to a thoroughfare that runs from the main road past the rear of the railway station. At the corner of the lane a Mr Antwiss, a Liverpool merchant, had a house with a large garden. A gardener named Walker was engaged to work there. This poor chap hanged himself one day, and his ghostly shade is said to haunt Walker's Lane, wandering up and down in the evenings.

A popular local custom was enjoyed by the youth of Little Sutton in Victorian times in early May when Chester's main race meeting was held. At this time many racegoers passing through the village stopped for refreshment at the Red Lion. The local lads would shout this rhyme

'Time, time, Chester Race time –
Cracking nuts and drinking wine.'

As the carriages departed some of the occupants would throw coins on to the carriage steps. If any boy attempted to take this bounty his hat would be hooked off by the racegoers with a stick. The lad would then chase after the coach and eventually his hat would be returned together with a generous contribution inside. It is said that some boys could make up to five shillings on Chester Race days.

⌘ LOWER PEOVER

References to Lower Peover made in the Domesday Book of 1086 suggest that the area was of little value and mostly 'waste'. A somewhat different picture exists today!

The church of St Oswald founded in 1269 and of Cheshire 'magpie' construction with a Norman sandstone tower, dominates the area. Its medieval bible chest was hewn from a Cheshire oak tree. Lower Peover Hall Farm (a manor house) is mentioned in records dated 1350.

The Warren de Tabley Arms, now known as The Bells, has been an inn since 1569. Prior to the building of the church, services were held by a monk from the mother church of Great Budworth who would stay in a dwelling which existed on

St Oswald's church, Lower Peover

the site of the present hotel. The landlord in 1871 was a George Bell whose family were brewers of beer on the premises and owners of several public houses in the area. His ghost is reputed to haunt the present beer cellar.

⌘ LOWER WITHINGTON

Lower Withington village forms the southern section of the manor of Old Withington, which was acquired around 1266 by a descendant of the Baskervyles who came over from Normandy with William the Conqueror in 1066. The estate was sold in 1960 to Mr E. Crosby, who rebuilt Withington Hall.

Adjoining the Park is Catchpenny Lane – so called because it was used by travellers to avoid paying the toll at Dingle Bank, and therefore a second toll bar was erected to catch the penny charge!

Cheshire Hunt Farm was at one time an inn and the Cheshire hounds were kennelled there. It is now owned by the University of Manchester and has been refurbished to accommodate post-graduate students studying for higher degrees at the Nuffield Radio Astronomy Laboratories, Jodrell Bank (founded by Sir Bernard Lovell in 1945) where the giant radio telescope was built in the 1950s.

The village green, known locally as the 'Sandhole', is a popular picnic area. Formerly it was used for horse racing during the annual Wakes week in November. Frumenty, consisting of boiled wheat and milk, was eaten by everyone during the Wakes.

In 1808 the Methodist chapel was built and still plays a prominent part in village life, often combining with St Peter's church (built 1892) to celebrate special events in the Christian calendar. Rogation Sunday is one such event when both the vicar and minister walk the local fields with their congregations, blessing the fields and the animals and crops in them.

The discovery of silica sand in Withington resulted in vast quantities being extracted for use in the glass-making, steel, and associated industries leaving several large water-filled quarries which have been landscaped and now form attractive wildlife sanctuaries.

⌘ LYMM

'Lime' is the version used in the Domesday survey, and the settlement was evidently well established by then. The present parish church of St Mary the Virgin is the fourth known to have been built on the same site, a grassy mound above the village itself.

Lymm's best known landmark is its ancient cross, set on steps carved in part from a natural outcrop of the local sandstone, geographically and culturally at the heart of the community. Through the years, the cross has been at the centre of all festivities old and new. The present day May Queen and Rushbearing processions

The market cross at Lymm

pass by it, the old Horse's Head plays and November Pig Fair were held there, and on Christmas Eve crowds of people gather to sing carols.

Until about 1700 most people made their living on the land but, as the population grew, other work was needed. Quarrying for building stone deepened the existing valley. Dams were built and the resulting water power was harnessed to drive mill wheels. A slitting mill cut brittle sheets of cast iron into strips for making nails and barrel hoops.

Around 1770 the Bridgewater Canal was extended from Worsley to Runcorn, cutting through Lymm and altering the village centre beyond recognition. This brought benefits in the form of quicker and cheaper transport which in turn boosted local industries, particularly fustian cutting. Fustian was a rough cotton cloth known as 'poor man's velvet'.

In 1824 the dam below the church was strengthened for the new turnpike road (now A56). This flooded the marsh near the church to create the large natural-looking lake, Lymm Dam.

More changes came with the railway and the Ship Canal. Wealthy Manchester families moved to Lymm, building large houses and bringing businesses and jobs. Several local industries flourished, notably basket making, salt production and gold beating. Gold leaf from Lymm embellishes the Dome of the Rock in

Jerusalem, the high altar of St Paul's Cathedral and, of course, our own village church.

⌘ MACCLESFIELD FOREST

'Macclesfield Forest' once meant a vast medieval hunting area for royalty but is now usually taken to mean the township, an area of scattered farms and in the centre a cluster of four buildings which formerly included the church, school, parsonage and pub. No visitor to this isolated hamlet would guess that in years past the place was humming with activity when royalty visited their hunting lodge.

The Forest Chapel in Macclesfield Forest

The church, or Forest Chapel is situated at about 1,300 ft above sea level. It was built in 1673 and rebuilt in 1834. It is well known for its annual Rushbearing Service, held on the Sunday after August (the Glorious) 12th when the current Lord Derby was likely to be staying at Crag Hall. Centuries ago rushes were strewn on church floors for warmth. Once a year these were ceremoniously renewed. Nowadays the chapel is decorated with plaited rushes and flowers and rushes are symbolically scattered on the floor. In 1848 windows had to be repaired in both church and school after 'a memorable Rushbearing'. In contrast a note in the register records that 'John Etchells did very meanly order only one bottle of Communion wine' and there was none left for Easter. Other entries record deaths in the snow: one, as recently as 1939, occurred at Christmas time and was not discovered until early March.

⌘ MALPAS

Malpas is a small township in a mainly agricultural area situated about 15 miles from Chester and six miles from Whitchurch, Shropshire, along the Roman road linking Chester with Wroxeter. The route formed a once much-disputed border between Cheshire and Wales.

Behind the church (St Oswald's) is a green mound which was the site of a small

Malpas, with the church steps on the left

Norman castle. The 14th century church has two chapels, one dedicated to the Brereton family and the other to the Cholmondeley family, both having featured widely in local history.

Malpas has a number of interesting buildings namely the Market House with its Tuscan columns, the tithe barn, a 17th century building, and the Cholmondeley almshouses built in 1721.

The Red Lion Inn is an old coaching inn visited by King James I in 1624. In the inn is a chair used by the King on this visit. It is a tradition that anyone sitting on this chair must pay one penny for the privilege or pay for a round of drinks for all present in the bar. However, the chair has had to be removed from the bar for its own protection since too many people were prepared to spend the penny and the chair was not up to it!

The Alport family of Overton Hall is remembered by the endowment of £500 to endow a Blue Coat charity school. The present primary school perpetuates their name.

Another notable figure, born in the Higher Rectory in 1783, was Reginald Heber who later became the Bishop of Calcutta. During his life he composed many hymns, perhaps the best remembered being *Holy, Holy, Holy* and *From Greenland's Icy Mountains*.

⌘ MARTON

The old village of Marton with its distinctive black and white church is situated on the A34 about four miles from Congleton. Its name derives from a large mere which was drained in the mid 19th century.

Sir John de Davenport granted the estates to his son Vivian and endowed the church in 1343. Effigies of both are in the church porch. The church, dedicated to St James and St Paul, is amongst the oldest of the black and white churches still in use in Europe. During restoration in the 19th century, medieval wall paintings were discovered on the west wall.

In the centre of the village is the Davenport Arms Inn – local justice used to be dispensed there and the local constable had to report periodically on the state of the stocks and pinfold. The Davenport family were Master Sergeants of Macclesfield Forest with power of life and death over malefactors, and their crest, of a felon's head with a rope round his neck, is still on the gable end of some of the properties.

William Buckley, born in 1780, was transported to Australia for taking part in a mutiny. He escaped prison camp on landing and spent the next 32 years with a tribe of aborigines. At 6 ft 6 inches he must have towered over the tribesmen, and had almost forgotten how to speak his native tongue. He died in 1856, aged 76, after falling from a horse. Buckley's Cave and Buckley's Falls in Australia are named after him, also the saying 'doing a Buckley'.

A local custom is the Gooseberry Show, one of the oldest in Cheshire. In 1978

The church of St James & St Paul, Marton

the largest gooseberry on record was entered in this show, and in 1987 the world record runner up was grown by a Marton man.

⌘ MICKLE TRAFFORD

Mickle Trafford is divided from Bridge Trafford by the river Gowy and derived its name from the ford which crossed the river in olden days. It is in the parish of Plemstall, which also includes the villages of Bridge Trafford, Picton, Picton Gorse, Hoole Bank, Hoole Village and part of Pipers Ash.

Plemstall church stands on a site where Christian worship has taken place since at least the 7th century. A legend tells of a shipwrecked fisherman who, during the height of a storm, made a vow that if he ever reached dry land he would build a church as an act of thanksgiving and dedicate it to St Peter the fisherman. At that time the area was marshland and tidal. Having found refuge on an outcrop of rock he built his church there.

Another place of interest in the village is the watermill, one of several astride the river Gowy between its source at Beeston and its outlet into the river Mersey. During the 1950s the mill ceased to be a privately owned working mill and was taken over by the Water Authority, who allowed it to become rather derelict. However, in the late 1970s and early 1980s a trust was formed and it has now been restored.

One resident of the parish with great claim to fame was John Hurleston of Picton Hall, whose family owned Picton and part of Upton. He is believed to have sailed with Drake against the Spanish Armada in 1588 and his portrait was on a postage stamp commemorating the 400th anniversary of the defeat of the Armada.

⌘ MINSHULL VERNON

On either side of the busy A530, midway between Nantwich and Middlewich, lies the scattered village of Minshull Vernon.

The land is mainly pasture and in former times the area was known for its cheese making. It boasts two greens, Bradfield and Whalleys, and it is from Bradfield Green farm that evidence of a settlement much earlier than the Norman period was found when police frogmen diving in the large water-filled pit there, discovered a bridge and road thought to be Roman. This road travels due north and another section of it was uncovered when restoration work was being carried out on the old vicarage.

The parish church of St Peter, erected in 1847 to replace an older one, was designed by Sir Gilbert Scott to seat 200. There is also a Congregational chapel, erected in 1809, and a Wesleyan chapel, built in 1832.

One inhabitant recalled the fun that they had roping after a wedding. As the bride and groom came down the road a rope was suddenly pulled in front of them and the perpetrators requested a coin as ransom before the happy couple were allowed to proceed. Not always did the ropers encounter a happy couple. On one remembered occasion the registrar from Nantwich, who was also a pig farmer, brought the wrong licence to the chapel so the marriage could not take place. However the couple were reassured to know that the registrar's pigs had a licence to prove that they were free from infection!

⌘ MOBBERLEY

Mobberley lies about 15 miles south of Manchester between Wilmslow and Knutsford. It existed centuries before it was mentioned in the Domesday Book under the Anglo-Saxon name of Motburleg. Originally it was all forest, but part of it was cleared by the Romans who built a road through what is now the village. The first church was built about AD 750 soon after the death of St Wilfrid, to whom it was dedicated. The present church of St Wilfrid was started in 1245.

Because of its long history and the large area it covers, Mobberley has many beautiful and interesting old buildings, some in typical Cheshire black and white, some with thatched roofs and cruck frames, and some in attractive weathered brick. Mobberley Old Hall, built in 1612, is a splendid building with mullioned windows standing in extensive gardens behind an ancient yew hedge. Saltersley

Farm is believed to be the oldest house in Mobberley and has been inhabited for over 600 years.

An old tradition, which dates from the time of the manorial court, is the election by the parish council of two burleymen. These were still called in to assess any damage done to crops or private property by straying cattle, and although their assessment was not legally binding, it was usually accepted by both sides.

⌘ MOORE

Moore and the hamlet of Keckwick lie in the Mersey valley, 100 ft below the gently sloping hills to the south-east, on the Runcorn road. Passing through also are two railway lines and the Bridgewater Canal, but they are now separated by part of the Runcorn New Town expressway.

The plantation of firs on Keckwick Hill was cleared just after the Second World War, but has been replanted. The quarry on the same hill was largely filled in so that the new Chester road could be built.

Most of the land has been drained and farmed for centuries. The Manchester Ship Canal now forms the northern boundary of Moore. The main Runcorn road probably followed the driest route along the valley, and slopes gradually from about 100 to 40 ft above sea level. All the older buildings are on or near this road. The central part of the village from Manor Farm to Canal Side Cottages is a conservation area, and many trees carry preservation orders. Strangely there were four farms within 50 yards of each other in the centre, and a fifth at the corner with Moss Lane, a short distance away. Of these, only two are now working farms – Manor Farm which dates from 1660, and Rose Farm, bearing a picture of a shire horse above the front door as these are bred by the owner.

Moore Hall, said to be haunted, with its fine late 17th century frontage, also stood very close to the main road, in the angle with Hobb Lane, but was split off from the road by the Bridgewater Canal in the 1760s. This canal, the earliest in Britain, closely followed the 100 ft contour in order to avoid locks. It runs parallel to the road until it reaches the Hall grounds, then swings away through the fields. The little bridges over it are rather too narrow for modern traffic.

⌘ MOTTRAM ST ANDREW

In 1086 a Saxon named Gamel is recorded as holding land in Motre. By 1414 the village was called Mottram St. Andrew. St. Andrew's Well is in Mottram Wood, from which the Old Hall was supplied with water.

Seams of copper and lead extending from the Alderley Edge mines produced a rich deposit of vanadium, a rare metal used in the hardening of steel. The ore was given the name Mottramite, and was discovered by Professor Roscoe in 1877.

Mottram Cross, an old butter cross, has a 14th century base and a restored shaft and head, dated 1832, bearing the coat of arms of the Wright family. There are accounts of bull baiting taking place, and a story that the steps served as an auction block when a husband wearied of his wife.

Across the road is the Bull's Head Inn, once a farm with a six day licence to sell liquor. The sign of a bull's head over a crown is the crest of the Wrights of Mottram.

St. Peter's church, Prestbury, is the parish church for Mottram, so many of the stones bear the names of Mottram families. The Greens occupied one old house for many years, and the epitaph to Ed, stonemason and parish constable, who was shot by a poacher, reads:

> Beneath this Stone lyes Ed Green
> Who for cutting Stone famous was seen
> But he was sent to apprehend
> One Joseph Clark at Kerridge End
> For stealing Deer of Esquire Downs
> Where he was shott and dyd o'th wounds.

⌘ MOW COP

Rising to 1,100 ft above sea level, Mow Cop, or Moel Coppa, has been interpreted as 'bald head', 'lofty summit', or 'hill of the cairn'. At one end of the Staffordshire

Mow Cop at sunset

Way, at least six counties can be seen from the Castle, which stands on the Staffordshire/Cheshire border. Sandstone was quarried here as far back as Roman times, and the cut-out shapes of millstones, or querns, can still be seen. The softer rock was pounded into sand for glass making. Stone walls were well in evidence, and the inhabitants of the stone cottages were, through the ages, quarrymen, smallholders and miners.

The Odd Fellows public house had the Staffs/Cheshire boundary running through it, so that at closing time, the customers moved over to the side which permitted another half hour drinking time. The same building, once a fustian mill, now manufactures surgical supplies.

In the wall by the Wesleyan chapel at The Bank and in the alley behind Westfield Road, were communal bread ovens, which were used in turn by the cottagers. Of the numerous wells and springs, many are no longer in use, or they have been covered over. It is claimed that the source of the Trent is here, and not at Biddulph Moor.

The stretch of Top Station Road by the Cheshire View Inn has a 1 in 3 gradient, where Foden's tested their lorries. Cycling and motor-cycle races also took place up Station Road. This same steep slope is now part of the 'Killer Mile' race which starts at the former station and ends at the Castle. It is an annual event and each April finds more contestants participating.

⌘ NESS & LITTLE NESTON

Ness Gardens has always been the hub of local social activity, going back to the end of the 19th century before Mickwell Brow was built in 1899 for the founder of Bees Nurseries. On that Brow many meetings were held by the villagers. The nursery moved to Sealand in 1913 and Mr Bulley then developed the land as his private garden open to the public day and night, free of charge, and called Ness Gardens.

In the early part of the 20th century, the colliery situated on the Ness coastline was the biggest employer of labour, and caused serious unemployment at its closure in 1926. The land and the village smithy were also a source of employment – the latter known as 'The Providence Works', and owned by a keen Methodist, Mr Joseph Mealor.

The house where Lady Hamilton, mistress of Lord Nelson, was born still remains and is the tall house at the end of the village named Swan Cottage. Her father was a blacksmith at the village smithy.

Mr Arthur Behrend lived at Friends Hall and was a member of the Liverpool shipping firm, Barr, Behrend & Co. He wrote *The House of the Spaniard*, a tale of mystery and intrigue inspired by Denna Hall, which is situated overlooking the Dee marshes.

A line of roughly hewn rocks on the fringe of the marsh was the only landing stage from the river Dee in the Denhall area. The Old Quay was the home of

The Botanic Gardens, Ness

smugglers and a landing place for Irish immigrants making their way along the marsh and Well Lane on their way to Chester.

⌘ ODD RODE

The district known as Odd Rode is made up of several small villages, namely Scholar Green, Kent Green, Mow Cop and Rode Heath. Running through the area is the Macclesfield canal, now mainly used for recreation, but in earlier times used to carry goods from the Potteries to Macclesfield.

Within its boundaries are the estates of Rode Hall, Ramsdell Hall, Little Moreton Hall and Lawton Hall. The property now known as Rode Hall was bought from the Rode family by Roger Wilbraham towards the end of the 17th century. In 1864 the then Squire Wilbraham was responsible for the building of All Saint's church, Odd Rode. Three schools were also founded by the Wilbrahams.

In the grounds of Lawton Hall is an unusual memorial stone. The inscription on the stone says – 'On the death of a bullfinch that sang God Save the Queen when bidden to do so'.

Close to Mow Cop station is Ransdell Hall, where a salt stream runs through the grounds and is supposed to possess healing powers. It is said the bargees used to collect their drinking water from it. Adjacent to the Hall is the coach house, where a

Little Moreton Hall at Odd Rode

'walk-in' ice house can be seen in the garden – used in times past for the cooling of wine and desserts.

About two miles from Scholar Green is Little Moreton Hall, built in the 15th and 16th centuries. It is one of the most perfect examples of a timber-framed, moated Elizabethan manor house and boasts a wainscoted gallery, a chapel, a great hall and a knot garden.

⌘ OLLERTON & MARTHALL

The villages of Ollerton and Marthall are situated two miles south of Knutsford and equidistant from Altrincham, Macclesfield, Northwich and Wilmslow. They are bounded by the hostelries, the Dun Cow to the north and the Egerton Arms to the south. The Dun Cow inn housed passing travellers and still has its water trough and mounting block.

The Egerton Arms marks the extent of the original Tatton estate and Lord Egerton's coat of arms can be seen on a farm in School Lane, Ollerton. He was considered to be a good landlord and farmers in the area were pleased when they were chosen to manage one of his farms. On days when they went to pay their rent, they could always rely on being provided with a good dinner in the tenants' hall at Tatton.

The A537 runs through the villages and was at one time a toll road with a turnpike gate at the Ollerton crossroads. It has always been a busy road, being a main route from the Mersey basin across the Pennines. One of the toll bar cottages, dated 1740, still remains.

The church of All Saints at Marthall was built in 1839. Before then the villagers were buried in Over Peover churchyard, and a bridle way which runs through Bowden Bank Farm was known as Coffin Walk as this was the route the coffins were carried to their last resting place.

A sizeable farming community remains with many farms passing from father to son. Part of a farm in School Lane has been made into a nature reserve with facilities for instruction for school parties.

⌘ OVER PEOVER

In early records Peover is spelt 'Peeffer', the original Anglo-Saxon meaning 'a bright river'. The river, though small, provided the mainstay of the villagers' diet

Tatton Hall, Ollerton

– trout – which can still be caught today in the same river, known as Peover Eye. The village of Over Peover, originally and still sometimes referred to as Peover Superior, has a population of about 700.

The Mainwaring family, who lived at Peover Hall, can be traced back over 500 years and it is thought that they originally came to the area in the time of Edward I; monuments to them are to be found in the church. The Mainwaring crest, which is used as the village emblem, is an ass's head. Legend tells the story that a Mainwaring's horse was shot at the Siege of Jerusalem. He could find only an ass to ride, so he rode into the city on this animal, saying 'Onward if I can', if Christ could ride on an ass so could he. This story was recognised by the Royal College of Heralds, who agreed to the words 'Devant si je puis' (Onward if I can) being the family motto and the ass's head being the family crest. It is to be found on numerous Mainwaring effigies in the church and also elsewhere in Cheshire.

Two buildings which attract visitors are the church of St Lawrence and Peover Hall, which stand close together in Peover Park. The older of the two is the church which dates back to 1450, although very little remains of the original structure and the main building was rebuilt in 1811. The Mainwaring family, who lived at Peover Hall, can be traced back over 500 years and it is thought that they originally came to the area in the time of Edward I.

Another famous resident of Peover Hall was General George Patton of the United States Army, who lived there during the Second World War. To this day the Stars and Stripes hangs with the Union Jack in the church of St Lawrence.

All good villages have a ghost and Over Peover is no exception. Where the Hall stands today there was once a monastery and legend has it that a monk walks the banks of Peover Pool saying his rosary and at midnight walks along Long Hey Lane by Black Pits and opens the gate.

Still very much a farming region, the number of commuters has grown over the years but Over Peover still retains very much a village feeling.

⌘ PARKGATE

Parkgate's name derives from Neston Park, which was enclosed in about 1250 and served as a deer park for 350 years. The river shore by Neston Park was recorded as one of several anchorages where ships would unload their goods if they were too large to reach Chester. In 1610 a sailor was arrested for smuggling calfskins, which were being exported without the necessary licence, from Chester to Parkgate – the first use of this name so far discovered.

The village was firmly established by 1720, and throughout that century Parkgate was renowned as the terminal for packet ships which carried passengers to Dublin. Travellers of all types, from the Lord Lieutenant of Ireland to Irish labourers, would wait here for a favourable wind.

The improvement of roads to Holyhead, where the sea journey was half the

From the marsh at Parkgate

distance, caused the Parkgate packet service to die in about 1810. Before then the village had become a seaside resort, and it continued to prosper until the 1830s. Parkgate then had to struggle to survive as a fishing village. Its fortunes revived when it began to be a residential area, and it now attracts both residents and visitors.

⌘ PECKFORTON

Peckforton is four miles south of Tarporley, on the eastern side of the sandstone ridge that runs across the Cheshire Plain.

The village, which has only a village room, a telephone box and a finger post to

Peckforton Castle (right) faces Beeston Castle

indicate its centre, sprawls out along three lanes leading to Beeston, Spurstow and Bulkeley. The oldest houses are black and white, square timber-framed on sandstone plinths. Some of the cottages are named according to their purpose or position – hence Parkgate, Laundry Cottage, Smithy Cottage and Garden Cottage. Fountain Cottages are called after a pub of that name demolished long ago. On the other hand, Elephant and Castle is not called after a pub, but takes its name from the sculpture in its front garden.

In 1840 the estate was bought by John Tollemache, who already owned much land in the district. Almost immediately he started to build Peckforton Castle on the end of a sandstone ridge facing Beeston Castle. Designed by Anthony Salvin, it is described by Pevsner as 'the facsimile of a very grand 13th century castle, correct and substantial enough to deceive anyone'. It was finished by 1851 at a cost of £67,847 9s 7$\frac{1}{2}$d.

He was created Baron Tollemache of Helmingham in 1876 in recognition of his services to agriculture. He had rebuilt or renovated the farmhouses and cottages, equipping each of the latter with a pigsty – in some cases very close to the back door! It was at this time that Peckforton buildings acquired their distinctive cast-iron diamond-paned windows and large chimneys.

⌘ PICKMERE

Pickmere lacked the large deposits of salt which attracted the Romans to Northwich but there are traces of a Roman road through one corner of the village. In 1274 the mere was referred to as Pike Mere – and the pike are still there!

Until the end of the 19th century there was nothing more than a collection of a few scattered farms and some mainly thatched cottages gathered round communal wells. Thatch was at hand in the mere and bricks were made in the village from clay dug from deep pits behind Crown Farm and baked on the spot. Village names bear witness to this past. Spinks Lane was where the hazel 'spinks' were cut, which were used to pin down the thatching. Wellfield Close was the site of the village well. Frog Lane speaks for itself!

In the early part of the 20th century, Pickmere Lake became enormously popular as a holiday centre. There were boats for hire on the mere for fishing and sailing, over 300 wooden chalets sprang up around the lake. Day trippers from Manchester arrived in huge four-horse wagons which pulled up at the Red Lion. Others came by train and on a fine summer's day a stream of people walked from Lostock station and over the footpaths to Pickmere. Lemonade and tea and cakes were served by many of the local farms and cottages.

The lake at Pickmere

⌘ POTT SHRIGLEY

A curious name, and its origins are uncertain. It is a puzzle as to whether the landowning families brought their names with them to the settlement or took them from the locality. A popular theory seems to be that 'Pott' comes from an old word denoting a pool (the land is still low lying and marshy to the north-west of the church) and that 'Shrigley' denotes a clearing in the woodland.

The Shrigleys were the earliest landowners of note. In 1313 their estates passed by marriage to the Downes of Taxal, Worth and Sutton and for the next five centuries this family acted as local squires of this small outpost on the outskirts of east Cheshire.

Members of the Downes family are recorded as being responsible for building the church over a period of time in the 14th and 15th centuries. At first a private chapel, this later became the parish church of St Christopher. Two of the present peal of six bells are of pre-Reformation date, and a third, perhaps the original 'Great Bell', is dated 1603.

Agriculture, coal mining, stone quarrying, brick making and estate work have provided employment for villagers over the years. Farming and a variety of small-scale light industries on the site of the former brickworks are the modern day equivalent. Pott Shrigley is in the Peak District National Park.

Pott Shrigley in autumn

⌘ POYNTON

Poynton is a thriving commuter village, straddling the A523 and nestling in the foothills of the Pennines. It is still a village, with a Parish Council, a brass band and its own agricultural and horticultural show and sports club, originally sponsored by the then Lord Vernon over 100 years ago.

Poynton Park and Pool are among the beauty spots of the village, being the place in which The Towers, the manor house of the Vernon family, was situated. Sadly, when the estate was split up and sold, The Towers, a grand stone building, was pulled down and the Vernons continued to live at Sudbury Hall, which now belongs to the National Trust.

Until the 1930s Poynton was a coal mining village with the mines, the land and most of the property belonging to Lord Vernon. The majority of the menfolk were employed in the mines or on his estate. Nature and man together have removed all traces of the mines from the village.

The Groundwork Trust has done a magnificent job in developing the old gig railway inclines and the Macclesfield/Marple railway lines into pretty, wooded walkways known as the Middlewood Way. The towpaths of the canal have also been restored.

Poynton is a mixture of the old and the new and the old cottages built to house the miners (sometimes with a family of up to 13 children) are much sought after. Some of these gabled stone cottages were built with the same warm stone that was used for Poynton church. There is a long row of 25 brick-built houses in Park Lane, and in Anson Clough a row of whitewashed stone cottages with a little stream meandering through their gardens.

⌘ PRESTBURY

The picturesque village of Prestbury stands on the river Bollin, three miles from Macclesfield. Before the 13th century there was a monastic settlement, from which the parish derives its name – Preost-Burgh, Priest's Town.

The parish was very extensive, the church at one time exercising ecclesiastical jurisdiction over 35 townships. It was the mother church, the only one licensed for marriages until 1878. The present church, dedicated to St Peter, was built about 1220, and the tower with its eight pinnacles about 1480. In the churchyard are two old yew trees said to be over 600 years old.

Legend has it that Bonnie Prince Charlie's route from Manchester to Derby lay through Prestbury. In December 1745 the bells were rung joyfully when the Duke of Cumberland marched through Prestbury in pursuit of the Jacobite rebels whose army he eventually overtook and defeated at Culloden.

After the fasts of Lent, Easter Monday in the past was for relaxing, known as Lifting Day. A chair was placed in the middle of the street, and any woman seen

Prestbury high street

outdoors was placed in the chair and lifted up and down the street until she paid for drinks for those carrying her. She was then free to go on her way.

Some 18th century houses still in use had three storeys, the top floor being used to house weavers' hand-looms for the Macclesfield silk industry. The homeworkers walked to Macclesfield to collect the silk yarn, then after weaving, they would return with the finished material; this journeying was known as 'padding'.

⌘ PUDDINGTON

Puddington lies on the southern edge of the Wirral peninsula, with a population of about 350, and overlooks the Dee estuary. Known as Potitone in the Domesday Book, the village is in the parish of Burton, with which it has been linked from the earliest times. The village consists of a cluster of cottages lining the road, a few modern houses, some outlying farms and a large ancient house known as Puddington Old Hall. This is about 600 years old and was a moated manor in medieval times. Parts of the moat can still be seen.

The village's most famous family, who lived in this house, were the Masseys. It has been said that the first member of this ancient family was granted the lands around Puddington by William the Conqueror. After the Reformation the Masseys remained Catholic and suffered social ostracism as 'Popish recusants'. Their schoolmaster, John Plessington, who was an ordained priest, was arrested in 1679 and nine weeks later was hung, drawn and quartered at Boughton Cross, Chester. His remains were brought back to Puddington Old Hall for display to deter further 'traitors'. His head was displayed on a pole at Chester.

Another old building still stands in the Home Farm yard, just as it did years ago. This is the old pigeon house, or columbarium, as it was called. It was a source of fresh meat in the days when there was only salt meat in the winter.

The village today is a little oasis of quiet in Wirral.

In the village of Puddington

⌘ RAINOW

On the border of the Peak National Park, the village of Rainow is situated three miles to the east of Macclesfield on the Chapel-en-le-Frith road. Bounded by Kerridge Ridge on one side and the Buxton Road on the other it runs towards the moors and Pennines. The hills and stone buildings are a sharp contrast to the old brick and softer countryside of the Cheshire Plain.

James Mellor, born 1796, lived most of his life at Hough Hole House. A Methodist, farmer and stonemason, he became a reader of Emmanuel Swendenborg, a Swedish scientist and engineer, who claimed to have received revelations from God. He created the garden at Hough Hole House, building a chapel in the grounds and adding a burial ground; he cut and inscribed his own tombstone. The present owners have restored the house, and the Mellor Gardens, which tell the story of Bunyan's *Pilgrim's Progress*, are open to the public on occasional Sundays during the summer.

With the Industrial Revolution came the building of cotton mills and the sinking of coal mines. Stone had been quarried on the west side of Kerridge for hundreds of years but during this period demand increased and several new quarries were opened and the old ones extended. At the same time came the enclosure of common land.

The view from Kerridge Hill, near Rainow

When the Macclesfield canal and the railway both bypassed Rainow and cheaper coal became available from Staffordshire, industry in the village declined and consequently the population decreased as people moved away to find work.

The only mill still standing today is at Gin Clough. Stone is still quarried on a small scale and the last coal to be mined was in 1926.

⌘ RUDHEATH

It is difficult to envisage that at one time a lawless breed of men once roamed here, but Rudheath was one of three 'criminal sanctuaries' established in Cheshire by the Norman Earls of Chester. The large tracts of heathland and forest once covering Rudheath's now fertile farmlands were the ideal haunts for outlaws and highwaymen who preyed on unsuspecting travellers.

In the late 1770s with the advent of the Trent and Mersey Canal, a wharf and warehouse were built at Broken Cross and Rudheath was used to store goods shipped from Staffordshire via the canal. The goods were off-loaded from the barges and subsequently transferred by horse-drawn transport to the river Weaver at Northwich. The Old Broken Cross public house nearby had stabling for the horses which drew the barges.

A few yards further along the canal stands a smithy and cottage, the smithy is still in use doing mainly small engineering work. Both the public house and the smithy are over 200 years old. The stables now form part of the public house and pleasure craft use the moorings previously used by the barges.

In 1835 a chapel of ease was built in King Street not far from the Broken Cross and canal. This chapel became known as Rudheath church and in 1912 a chancel was added to the building.

⌘ SAUGHALL

When Chester was an important seaport, Saughall was a small settlement to the north-west where the villagers made a living by fishing. Constant silting up of the estuary and the later channelling of the river has meant that Saughall now looks out from the old Dee banks over the flat reclaimed area known as Sealand and is two miles from the river. Ponies from the nearby riding stables graze the banks upon which the fishermen must have dried their nets centuries ago.

Saughall today is a large village with a population of over 3,500, with several shops and modern housing estates grouped around the original core of village buildings, some of which are quite ancient – the Charity House is 16th century and partly built with stones from Shotwick Castle. Just below the Greyhound pub is a black and white timbered farmhouse dating from about 1560. The tithe barn at

Shotwick Lodge Farm is 15th century and its massive roof beams were hewn from oak from Shotwick Park. There is still a small area of woodland – a remnant of the once enclosed park.

The crossroads between Seahill Road, Church Road, Hermitage Road and the road to Shotwick House is the natural centre of the village. On the four corners stand the Greyhound pub, the vicarage where in June the annual ceremony of crowning the Rose Queen takes place in the lovely old walled garden, the Vernon Institute and the former 'Swinging Gate Inn' which dates back to 1490 but sadly relinquished its licence in the 1960s and became a private residence. The iron double manacle which used to be fastened to an oak beam in the bar parlour was used to hold prisoners by the wrists before they were taken off to Chester. This interesting relic is now housed in the Vernon Institute.

⌘ STRETTON

South of Warrington is the village of Stretton: the busy crossroads of the A49 London road, Hatton Lane and Stretton Road bisect it. Lights were installed to help control the traffic in 1975. Stretton is mainly agricultural, with dairy and arable farms, some with pedigree Friesian cattle.

Central to the village is St Matthew's church, built of sandstone in 1827. This has a Perpendicular western square tower built in 1870. From the top of the tower seven counties can be seen on a clear day. The six bells are rung each Sunday and at weddings. The church clock face was renewed in 1963 and reads on one side 'Time is not all' and on the other 'Forget not God'.

The Beehive Stores and post office, built of local sandstone, started business in the Mounfield family 1885. There are two public houses – one, the Cat and Lion, built of local sandstone. The sign built in a ring over the front door reads 'The Lion is strong, The Cat is Vicious – My Ale is good and so is my liquor'. Richard Braithwaite, self-styled Drunken Barnaby, called here in 1636 on his journey to Lancashire. The Ring O'Bells is in Lower Stretton, now the other side of the M56. These pubs had a tontine (savings) club, used chiefly by the Irish who came to work on the farms.

There are a number of listed buildings in Stretton, including Tanyard farm built in the late 17th century. A chain still hangs in the chimney that was used to cook the roast. The local smithy and wheelwright's in Common Lane, Lower Stretton, built in 1860 and owned by the Savage family, closed and was sold to a developer for housing.

⌘ STYAL

It is said the name 'Styal' meant 'the secret place', because when the taxmen of long ago came to check how many hectares of barley or wheat were being grown, the

Cottages at Styal

village was suspiciously silent and vacant. There is no proof of this, but it *is* a good story!

Apprentice House, home for children who worked in the cotton mill, was founded by the Greg family, who also built a school and two chapels as well as the cobbled streets, and indeed, the village itself. Down in the valley, washed and worked by the river Bollin, stands the mill.

The village is now owned by the National Trust and the mill contains a museum of the cotton industry.

Styal Cottage Homes once provided shelter for orphans and unwanted children. There were house mothers, a band and bandmaster, and an excellent record for their protégés in later life. Visitors come now and again and ask about people they knew when they had shelter in the Homes. It is currently a women's prison.

⌘ SUTTON

The parish of Sutton lies about three miles south of Macclesfield and falls naturally into three areas – Langley, Sutton Lane Ends and Lyme Green.

The Macclesfield Canal runs through Lane Ends and Lyme Green. It was opened for traffic on 10th November 1831 and connects the Trent and Mersey Canal, near Kidsgrove, with the Peak Forest Canal near Marple. Coal, salt, lime

Trout fishing at Ridgegate Reservoir, Sutton

and stone were the usual cargoes; now the canal provides pleasure for walkers and boaters alike and an important habitat for varied wild life.

The canal has a special significance in Sutton for it was here that James Brindley, of canal building fame, served as an apprentice to Abraham Bennett from 1733 to 1740. Brindley had a childhood interest in engineering principles and this natural talent was developed during his apprenticeship. The turning point of his career came when the Duke of Bridgewater appointed him chief engineer for the construction of his canal from Worsley to Manchester.

C. F. Tunnicliffe, OBE, RA, the country and bird life artist, was born in 1901 in

Langley where his father, William, was a shoemaker. By the time Charles was two years old the family had moved to a farm in Sutton Lane Ends. Stories are told of his early childhood drawings being found on fences and shippon walls.

Early in the 19th century the silk industry was started in Langley by William Smith. By the later years of the century the business had passed, through marriage, to the Whiston family. The fame of this company spread worldwide and it was acknowledged to be the largest hand-block printing, dyeing and finishing company in the world. Sadly, with changes in the textile world, 1964 saw the closure of the works and a change of identity in the village. However, a few years later, hand-block printing returned on a smaller scale in the hands of a new company.

⌘ TARPORLEY

The church, the manor house and the Swan Hotel are at the three points of a triangle and were the focal points of village life. The beautiful church, the south side of which commands a magnificent view of the castles and hills, dates from the 13th century, the failing structure being restored in early Victorian times. The old families of the Dones and the Earls of Haddington were generous benefactors. Indeed the parish hall, a listed building, is called the Done Room.

The Earl of Haddington founded the Tarporley Fire Brigade in 1869, when most fire brigades belonged to insurance companies. It was the first voluntary fire brigade in the country, and it still functions round the clock, manned by men who are in full-time work, and who provide cover at all times with modern equipment and the expertise of regular brigades – a great achievement.

The late 18th century, being an era of prosperity, meant that many of the timber-framed buildings were replaced with brick, as seen in front of the optician's where a brick is preserved dated '1796 S.S.', the S.S. being marked by fingers on wet clay. It was during this period that the front of the Swan Hotel was replaced by the present Georgian façade, although some of the older building still remains.

No doubt the oldest building of note is the manor house, rebuilt on the site of an older house dated 1585, as can been seen on the beam across the front. The house was placed at the left hand corner of the village triangle, the church being the apex, and it would appear that the village ended there, the later road swinging round the corner.

⌘ TARVIN

A battlemented church tower in mellow sandstone, cottages whose visible foundations are red rock, elegant Georgian residences, half-timbered houses, a centuries-old building originally the grammar school and brick dwellings of the

19th century – this is Tarvin, to which have been added many fine modern developments.

The village stands where the Nantwich and Manchester roads meet, five miles east of Chester and close to the old Watling Street, which must have echoed to the tramp of Roman legions in the first centuries of the Christian era. Nowadays, two bypasses enable the hurrying traffic to avoid the village centre.

St Andrew's, a lovely old parish church, incorporates a 14th century south aisle with its original roof, a 15th century tower and various additions from succeeding centuries. The manor house opposite the church suggests a link with the days when the Bishop of Lichfield was lord of the manor. Tarvin Hall, facing into the broad end of High Street, was rebuilt in brick in the Georgian style. In 1752, a disastrous fire destroyed many of the timber-framed cottages, hence the Georgian rebuilding still evident in the village centre.

Until the 1920s, there was a Tarvin souling play performed annually on All Souls' Eve. This comprised the usual exchanges between Saint, or King, George and his adversary, known in some areas as the Black Prince, but in Tarvin as the Cheshire Champion. Opening with the traditional souling song, one verse was exclusive to Tarvin, and was quoted in 1891 as:–

'Your lanes they are dirty, and your meadows grow cold,
And if you are willing with us you may go,
We will bring you safe back again, you have no need fear,
And it's all that we are souling for is your ale and strong beer.'

Tarvin is a busy and friendly village, proud of its historic roots and its energetic present.

⌘ TATTENHALL

Tattenhall lies approximately eight miles south-east of Chester on a slight rise in the ground between the river Gowy, which flows into the Mersey, and the Golbourne brook, which flows into the Dee.

Throughout the centuries several churches have stood successively on the same site and it is possible that there was a pagan shrine here. A skeleton was dug up near the north wall of the present church of St Alban, of a tall man who had a coin under his head, perhaps to pay his fare across the 'river of death'.

During the 19th century the churchyard was used by robbers who lived in caves in the nearby Peckforton Hills, from where they terrorised the villagers. They are reputed to have hidden their ill-gotten gains in the graves, which they also plundered. Isabella Bird, the rector of the day's daughter, caught them at it and was offered a black silk dress as 'hush-money'. However, her morals too were questionable, as she both accepted the dress and then also 'split' on them. William

Dean, known as the Tattenhall wizard, lived in a cottage here in the 19th century. The local children feared having one of his spells cast upon them. Another thing to fear was the ghost of a headless woman who was said to sit after dark by the Pool Head Field gate on the Chester Road. An old couplet runs:

> 'Coom thou yarly, coom thou leet
> Be weer of the Buggin at the Poo Yed Geet.'

There are now approximately 3,000 people living here. In 1763 there were only 692 inhabitants living in 149 households, but then came the Shropshire Union Canal which brought jobs and small industries. Next came the railway. Tattenhall actually had two stations, one on the Crewe/Chester line and the other on the Whitchurch/Chester line. This meant that businessmen from as far away as Liverpool could live here and yet easily reach their offices. It is said that one 19th century stationmaster would not let the train depart if he heard a commuter's pony and trap hurrying along the road. Neither station exists now but the canal is much frequented by pleasure boats.

⌘ THORNTON HOUGH

Thornton Hough is situated in the middle of the Wirral peninsula. The village was called Torintone in the Domesday Book. In the reign of Edward II it was held by Roger de Thornton, whose only daughter became the wife of Richard del Hoghe, hence the name Thornton Hough.

Thornton Hough chiefly evolved through the work of two enterprising men. Joseph Hirst, a Yorkshire woollen manufacturer from Wilshaw near Huddersfield, came here in the mid 1860s to retire, and built his home, Thornton House, All Saints' church and vicarage, and a village school which is now the church hall. Two years later he built the village stores and a row of stone cottages named Wilshaw Terrace. An unusual feature of the parish church tower is a fifth clock face high on the north aspect, so that Joseph Hirst could see it from his bedroom window.

The second person to complete the major part of this purpose-built village was William Hesketh, later the first Viscount Leverhulme, who came from Bolton in 1887 to set up a new soap factory in Port Sunlight. He bought Thornton Manor, later extending this Victorian house into what is now a neo-Elizabethan stately home. He also built the post office and village club together with the school which is still in use today.

The village has a most attractive village green of some 14 acres surrounded by half-timbered black and white houses, all in different styles.

⌘ TILSTON

Tilston as a village dates from Saxon times and it comprises the four townships of Stretton, Carden, Horton and Grafton. Ormerod describes it as 'one of the most important and populous villages in the barony of Malpas'.

By 1346 the local landowner was John Leche who lived at Carden Hall. His son became leech or surgeon to Edward III from which time the family fortunes increased. Carden Hall, a beautiful timbered mansion, was burned down in 1912, after which the family moved to Stretton Hall.

In a cave in Carden Park lived a hermit who went around the villages preaching to anyone who would listen to him; while another old man lived in a shack near the village and the local people visited him to be cured of warts.

The church dating back to the 14th century was the centre of village life and the custom of rushbearing still continues; so does the annual Wakes where the ox-roast takes place, the first slice being auctioned and sold to the highest bidder.

Originally there were four public houses in Tilston: The Cape of Good Hope, the Fox and Hounds, the Butcher's Arms (now an antiques shop) and the Carden Arms. The Carden Arms was run at one time by Teddy Carlton, who put on music hall shows in Chester.

Tilston school was opened in 1872 on land given by Mr Leche; attendance was erratic, children being absent helping with the harvest, crow scaring, stone picking, fruit gathering, picking acorns and blackberries. A new extension to the school was built in 1976.

⌘ WAVERTON

Waverton, spelled Wavretone in the Domesday Book 1086, is situated four miles south-east of Chester. It was largely a farming community, there being 14 farms, of which only five now remain, the greater portion of the old village being part of the Eaton estate.

The foundation date of the church of St Peter is uncertain, but it is probably that a church was here in Saxon times. The church is built of red sandstone taken from the nearby quarry. The Tudor doorway at the west end is notable for its square frame with curved shields of the Duttons and Hattons in the spandrels. Both corners of the frame are decorated with two headless figures, probably angels. Legend says that Cromwell's soldiers beheaded them during their purge of images from churches.

The Ellesmere and Chester Canal built in the 18th century (now the Shropshire Union Canal) cuts across the village and is spanned by many bridges now listed as being of historic importance.

In 1662 Jonathan Barker left £2 10s, while in 1702 Elizabeth Dutton left 'to the Poor of Waverton' the interest of £30 'to be paid on New Year's Day for ever'. In

Along the Shropshire Union Canal at Waverton

1706 Richard Ralphson left the sum of £5, 'the Interest to be paid out in Bread to be distributed at Easter and Christmas yearly for ever'. The interest from these legacies, and the Sarah Bevan Charity, is still, to this day, distributed to the needy in Waverton.

⌘ WEAVERHAM

Weaverham was an important place at the time of the Domesday survey and even owned seven salt houses in nearby Northwich. Some Roman finds have been made suggesting that there may have been a farming community here at that time. In the middle ages, the village belonged to the Vale Royal Abbey.

The last battle of the Civil War took place in the parish and ended with the Royalists' defeat at Winnington Bridge.

The beautiful 15th century tower of St Mary's parish church can be seen from all points of the village, and from it a splendid peal of bells rings out each Sunday. The church was mentioned in the Domesday Book (as were the Salt House Meadows and possible salt workings).

A carved stone slab, found in the churchyard, is thought to be of pagan origin. This is now mounted and can be seen in a side chapel. In the late 19th century a Virgin's Club (so called because the church was dedicated to the Virgin Mary) met yearly in the old thatched cottage in West Road. The members wore white and marched to a service in the church, followed by a meal in the Star Inn.

Weaverham people are known as Russets (named after a local apple), as in the old rhyme 'Weaverham Russets, Crowton Crabs, Norley Gawbys, Acton Good Lads'.

One village character was Captain Hatton, who was responsible for the law on hanging to be changed. The old law stated that a man should be hanged for one hour and his body given to his friends. Captain Hatton was arrested and hanged for piracy at the beginning of the 19th century. But he inserted a silver tube into his throat and survived. The law was then reworded that 'a man shall be hanged by the neck until he be dead'.

Poplar Cottage, a 17th century thatched cottage in the centre of the village, had a room on the ground floor called the 'Birth Chamber', where village mothers could enter by an outside door to give birth to their children. This followed an old superstition, that to rise in the world a newborn child must first be carried upstairs.

It is interesting to note that Weaverham well was an open spring which never ran dry. It was the only source of water for some houses well into the 20th century, and was credited with healing powers. It was believed that any visitor who drank the water, was bound to return.

⌘ WILDBOARCLOUGH

The 24th May 1989 is a day that will never be forgotten by the villagers of Wildboarclough, when vast devastation was caused by a flash flood sweeping through the valley. The early afternoon turned black as night as a tremendous thunderstorm approached. Torrential rain overloaded Clough brook, which raged through the village uprooting trees, sweeping away stone walls, destroying bridges, and carrying cattle miles along the valley. The postman arriving to collect the late afternoon mail was unable to do so as the post-box had completely disappeared and has yet to be found! Their are earlier records of such deluges, suggesting that Wildboarclough is aptly named 'the wild stream in the valley'.

Unlike most Cheshire villages Wildboarclough, remotely situated on the Pennine foothills, has deep sheltered valleys and bleak upland moorlands. With the coming of the textile revolution in the 18th century and the need for water power, the Clough brook in a narrow section of the valley attracted George Palfreyman over the border from Staffordshire. Around 1800 he established the Crag Works for calico printing, Crag Hall for his own residence, and several cottages for the workers.

There are thin seams of poor quality coal under the hills, some only about two feet thick thick. These were last worked about 50 years ago by miners lying on their sides to attack the face.

Today sheep farming is the main industry in Wildboarclough, and a sheep sale

The moorlands above Wildboarclough

is held in the village every autumn.

> There once was a man from Clough
> Who said: 'I have had quite enough!
> From Wincle to Sutton
> There's nothing but mutton,
> And I'm heartily sick of the stuff!'

⌘ WILLASTON-IN-WIRRAL

This village in the heart of Wirral was first mentioned by name in 1230. Although

The restored railway station at Willaston-in-Wirral

not recorded as a settlement in the Domesday Book, it gave its name to the Hundred of Wilaveston, or Wirral. When the hundred comprised both the peninsula and the townships right up to the city of Chester, the hundred court was held here.

The substantial farmhouses built around the village green in the 17th and 18th centuries are of brick, with stone dressings, some incorporating older parts in half-timbering or stone. The most imposing is Wallaston Old Hall, with an Elizabethan-style façade.

The green forms a focus of village life, and was secured for future generations by registration in 1983. One picturesque event held there until recently was the Boxing Day meet of the Royal Rock Beagles, the oldest pack in England. The adjacent Memorial Hall is home to many local organisations.

Willaston was one of seven townships of the parish of Neston until its own church was built in 1855. It became independent in 1865, with its own parish registers. The first burial entry was for Charity Taylor, a gypsy girl who died when camping nearby. For many years afterwards, her family ceremonially visited her grave.

The windmill, the tallest in Wirral, which was built in 1800, once provided employment for up to 40 people, but has not worked since 1930. During the Second World War, it was a lookout post for the Home Guard. Now without sails, and converted into a private home, it is still the principal landmark of the village, and is the motif on the school badge, and on the guide posts of the village walks.

The first great change was the coming of the railway in 1866. Although only a single track between Hooton and West Kirby, it gave the farmers swift access to Liverpool and Chester, as well as the rest of Wirral. Milk could be sold directly, rather than as cheese, though the farms retained their cheese presses for the summer glut of milk. The line has now been converted into the Wirral Country Park, known as the Wirral Way, a twelve mile walk and bridleway. Hadlow Road station has been preserved exactly as it was in 1956 when the line closed.

⌘ WINCLE

Wincle school and St Michael's church

Surrounded by the hills of the Pennines and on the outer fringe of the Peak District National Park, the village of Wincle nestles on the banks of the Dane valley.

There was a church on the site of the present one in about the 11th century, when it was a chapel of ease. The present church was reconstructed in the mid 1600s, later modified by the Victorians in the 1880s. The school and the vicarage were built at the same time from the local sandy gritstone.

Wincle Grange, now a farmhouse, was a Cistercian property in the 14th century with, it is said, an underground passageway to the chapel of ease.

When Bonnie Prince Charlie rode out of Macclesfield with his army of faithful followers on his way south to capture the throne of England, he travelled through Wincle. He is said to have stopped at the Ship Inn, leaving behind his gun and other items. There is supposed to be a headless horseman who rides through the village and down the Dane valley on misty nights. Perhaps he was a lost supporter of Bonnie Prince Charlie, returning home after the defeat of the last battle.

⌘ WINSFORD

Winsford has no mention in the Domesday Book, but the villages of Over and Wharton were listed. Much of its history and growth is rooted in the salt mining industry. Salt mining still flourishes today with the only working rock salt mine in the UK. Winsford Flashes is a local beauty spot, arising from land subsidence through mine workings and subsequent flooding by the River Weaver. Today the Flashes are used for marine sports.

One of the oldest houses in Winsford is Dawk House dated 1711, and older still is Littler Grange Farm, part of which dates from the 16th century. Other buildings of interest are Brunner Guildhall, Verdin School, the old Free Library building and Church House Farm, formerly the medieval Blue Bell Inn.

Perhaps the most famous son is John Bradbury who was born in Winsford in 1872 and lived in the town until the age of 15. After moving away his career took him to the position of Chief Cashier at the Bank of England which he held when the very first issue of the old ten shilling and one pound notes was made. Both bore his signature, and consequently became nicknamed 'Bradburies'. John Bradbury never forgot the town of his birth as on elevation to the peerage he chose the name 'Lord Bradbury of Winsford'.

A local custom up until the 1960s was that of giving each child a present of a ball on Good Friday. The origins of this gift are unknown – other nearby towns and villages had never had such a custom.

⌘ WINWICK

In ancient times, to travel north through the bogs, mosslands and forests of the Mersey valley, it was necessary to ford the tidal river Mersey at Warrington and follow the trail through Winwick. Being of such strategic importance, it is not surprising to find within the parish a 3,000 year old Bronze Age burial barrow, a Roman road, one of the earliest Christian burial grounds circa AD 700 and, of course, the beautiful church of St Oswald.

The Winwick pig, is carved on the west wall of the tower, the oldest part of the church, next to statues of St Anthony and St Oswald. Legend has it that the church was to be built at the foot of the hill but, each night, a pig moved the stones to the top. This was seen to be an omen of such portent that the church was built at the top of the hill.

St Oswald, King of Northumbria, was killed in the battle of Maserfield on 5th August AD 642. As he lay dying, it is said that, in his agony, he scratched the soil. Where his fingers had touched, water appeared and, at the spot, a well was formed. It was discovered that the water of the well had miraculous properties curing people of illness and disease.

In 1547 there was a grammar school in Winwick, which closed its doors in 1890 due to lack of pupils. On the corner of Newton Road and Green Lane stood the old school house. This house contained the girls charity school. The boys charity school was opened in 1815.

⌘ WRENBURY

The earliest recorded mention of Wrenbury is in the Domesday Book of 1086. At that time, like much of south Cheshire, it was part of the lands held by William de Malbanc, who had come over with the Conqueror.

A church is first mentioned in the early part of the 12th century, and in those early days it was in the charge of the monks who had settled at Combermere Abbey, some four miles away. The present building was erected about 1500 with stone from the nearby Bickerton hills.

Every generation has left is mark on the building somewhere. It still has 17th century box pews. The crests on the pew doors are not those of the people who sat there, but of their landlords. From an old seating plan it appears that a seat in the church went with the tenancy of a particular farm, so that if a family moved to a different farm in the parish they had to move to a different pew as well!

One unusual feature is the Whipper's Pew just by the door. It was the seat of the dog whipper, who was not there to keep dogs out, but to keep in order those that were in! For this he was paid five shillings per year, and received a coat and hat from the parish too.

At the end of the 18th century, the Ellesmere canal was built through Wrenbury, which made it much easier to trade with Chester, North Wales and the Midlands. The railways came soon after, in the 1860s, when the line was built from Shrewsbury to the new railway town of Crewe. For the first time some of the villagers became 'commuters' to jobs in Crewe or Nantwich.

Today the canal has a brisk trade in holiday craft every summer, when the village looks a bit like a holiday resort!

⌘ WYBUNBURY

Wybunbury is in South Cheshire, roughly four miles south of Crewe and three miles south-east of Nantwich. It was a settlement established before the Norman Conquest and on early maps is shown as one of the most important places in Cheshire. The most common form of pronunciation nowadays seems to be 'Winbury'.

The church is dedicated to St Chad, first Bishop of Mercia who was canonised after his death in AD 672. Unfortunately, the site on which Wybunbury churches have stood is unstable due to the action of running, sand, salt and springs. Five churches have been built on the site, only to be demolished as they became unsafe. Of the 15th century church only the magnificent tower remains – 96 ft tall and a landmark for miles around. The tower has required attention over the years to correct a tendency to 'lean'. In the 18th century 'as crooked as Wimberie steeple' was a saying throughout the county. In 1833 James Trubshaw of Staffordshire built a new church and straightened the tower, by then nearly 6 ft out of true.

Half a century later the church was pronounced too dangerous for public worship and closed. Around 1893 another church was built. At the consecration a remark was made that 'Nothing but an earthquake will ever move Wybunbury church again'. Sadly, this confidence was misplaced – the church, the last on the site, was demolished in 1976.

A few years before, in 1968 the church was the scene of an amazing discovery when an iron chest, untouched for years in the tower, was opened. Inside were silver items dating from the 16th and 17th centuries, including a Charles II tankard, later sold and the £10,250 raised put towards a new church. This was built on a new site further along the main road and consecrated in 1978. When the tower itself was threatened with demolition, villagers formed a Trust Fund to save it.

Wybunbury is also famous for the nature reserve located to the north of the village. Wybunbury Moss covers 26 acres. In the centre is a deep and rather dangerous hollow filled with water on which floats a 'raft' of peat covered in sphagnum moss. Pine and birch trees and other plants add to this unique habitat – the home of many rare species of plants and other wildlife.